PRODUCTIVITY AGREEMENTS AND WAGE SYSTEMS

Productivity Agreements
and
Wage Systems

D T B North and G L Buckingham

Gower Press

First published in Britain by Gower Press Limited
140 Great Portland Street, London W1N 5TA
1969

Second impression 1969

Set in 10 on 12 point Times and printed by
Hazell Watson and Viney Ltd
Aylesbury, Bucks

Contents

Preface   xi

PART I: BACKGROUND TO PRODUCTIVITY BARGAINING

1 PRODUCTIVITY BARGAINING IN DEPTH   1
Need for comprehensive approach—Contents of a
comprehensive agreement: security of employment
plan; role specification and measurement; rational wages
system; communications structure; rules and procedures;
fringe benefits

2 EMPLOYEE MOTIVATION AND INDUSTRIAL RELATIONS   9
Traditional concepts of employee motivation—
Changing views of motivation—Hierarchy of needs—
Motivation–hygiene theory—Principle of supportive
relationships—Basic concepts of management–employee
relations—Restructuring the industrial relations
situation

PART II: CONDUCT OF THE FEASIBILITY STUDY FOR A PRODUCTIVITY AGREEMENT

3 SCOPE AND ORGANISATIONAL IMPLICATIONS   21
Area of investigation: company, plant, or
department—Problem of the large company:
creation of an industrial relations policy

4 PRODUCTION ANALYSIS 29

What to measure—How to measure—Activity
sampling—Effect of machine speeds on productivity—
Multiple regression analysis in the measurement of
work activities—Other measures

5 ECONOMIC ANALYSIS AND COSTING 41

Economic characteristics of the company—Sales and
market trends—Calculation of labour costs—Reduction
of overall costs

6 SOCIOLOGICAL ANALYSIS 50

Use of the attitude survey: examples of survey results—
Consultative machinery within the company—Evidence
of labour turnover—Other areas of investigation

7 ANALYSIS OF THE WAGE SYSTEM AND ITS EFFECTS 62

Need for a detailed wage analysis—Technique of wage
analysis—Differentials in the existing wage structure—
Effectiveness of existing incentive schemes

PART III: DESIGN AND DEVELOPMENT
OF A WAGE SYSTEM

8 CURRENT SYSTEMS 73

Effectiveness of payment-by-results systems—
PBR in action: Coventry "mutuality"—Measured
and controlled day-work—Graded hourly rates—
Plant-wide incentive schemes

9 MODEL PRINCIPLES 86

Expectations in common—Importance
of differentials—Variable element
in remuneration—Share-of-prosperity element—
Added value component

10 DESIGN OF COMPONENTS 96

Evaluation of job worth—Design of variable element
—Design of share-of-prosperity element

11 RATIONALISING A WAGE STRUCTURE   115

Defining a grade structure—Analysing the basis of
new grade structure proposals—Cost of rationalising
wage structure—Effect of incentive payments on
company costs

PART IV: INSTALLATION OF A
PRODUCTIVITY AGREEMENT

12 DEVISING THE AGREEMENT   131

Case for reducing overtime—Revision of working
hours—Labour flexibility—Reactions to work study—
Regulation of lateness and absenteeism—Staff status
and fringe benefits

13 MANPOWER PLANNING AND SECURITY OF EMPLOYMENT   144

Economic necessity for manpower planning—
Developing a security-of-employment plan

14 COMMUNICATIONS   151

Principles of industrial communications—Design
of a communications system

15 NEGOTIATION AND IMPLEMENTATION   163

Negotiation of agreement—Devising programme for
negotiation and implementation—Communicating
information about the agreement

PART V: AFTER THE AGREEMENT

16 IMPLICATIONS FOR MANAGEMENT   175

Managerial initiative and industrial relations policy—
New management style—Role of the foreman—Summary

17 IMPLICATIONS FOR TRADE UNIONS   183

Impact of national agreements—Role of shop
stewards—Role of union officials

18 CONCLUSION: MOVEMENT TOWARDS COMPREHENSIVE
PRODUCTIVITY AGREEMENTS   191

APPENDICES

1 IMPEDIMENTS TO PRODUCTION   197

2 MULTIPLE REGRESSION ANALYSIS   200

3 ATTITUDE SURVEY   204

4 CRITERIA OF THE PRICES AND INCOMES BOARD FOR A
SUCCESSFUL PAYMENT-BY-RESULTS SCHEME   210

5 ASSESSMENT FORM FOR A GRADED HOURLY RATE SYSTEM   212

6 EMPLOYMENT SECURITY PLAN   214

7 RECOMMENDED CONSTITUTION FOR A WORKS PRODUCTIVITY
COUNCIL   222

8 NOTES FOR THE GUIDANCE OF COMMITTEE CHAIRMEN,
REPRESENTATIVES AND ELECTORS   228

9 RECOMMENDED CONSTITUTION FOR A SUGGESTION SCHEME   231

10 RECOMMENDED APPEALS PROCEDURE   235

11 RECOMMENDED PROCEDURE FOR SETTLING DISPUTES   238

12 PROPOSALS FOR A PRODUCTIVITY AGREEMENT   240

13 PRODUCTIVITY AGREEMENT AND NEW SYSTEM OF
WAGE PAYMENT   242

14 SUPERVISORS' APPRECIATION AND TRAINING
PROGRAMME   252

Index   255

Illustrations

2:1 Hierarchy of human needs   12

2:2 Comparison of satisfiers and dissatisfiers   14

3:1 Schematic representation of the feasibility study   22

4:1 Measurement techniques shown diagrammatically   35

5:1 Examples of break-even charts and cost and profit
     calculation for three companies   43

5:2 Diagrams of break-even charts   44–5

6:1 Analysis of employee attitudes   55

6:2 Analysis of employee attitudes   56

7:1 Distribution of earnings: Company *A*   66

7:2 Distribution of earnings: Company *B*   67

8:1 Philips premium payment plan   79

10:1 Output grid showing job evaluation results for
     thirty-one job samples   103

10:2 Example of yield index   105

10:3 Relationship between pay bands and performance   108

11:1 Proposed grade structure: Company *A*   120

11:2 Proposed grade structure: Company *B*   123

11:3 Comparison of effects on bonus curves of different
     shares for time-saved schemes   125

11:4   Actual example of variations in wage costs
according to the share of labour costs savings
allocated to the work force   126

14:1   Integrated joint consultative structure   159

A9:1   Example of a notification slip   233

A13:1   Wage structure: build up of earnings   245

A13:2   Wage structure: individual bonus pay bands   247

Preface

This book has some pretensions, but not many. It does not claim to be an authoritative study of the development of productivity bargaining in Britain and its influence on the industrial scene, nor to speculate upon the relative importance of the various factors contributing to this development. These factors would, no doubt, include the state of the national economy and its influence upon the short- and long-term objectives of the political parties, the growth of technology and capital investment in manufacturing processes, social and educational improvements causing changed expectations of people towards their work situation, the organisation and influence of the trade unions, the development of managerial techniques and information systems—and many others.

It would also be misleading to claim it as a textbook in the sense of presenting well-authenticated techniques for the resolution of specific problems. Some techniques are presented which have been to a greater or lesser extent tested and found useful, but they are put forward in the context of their possible application within a problem-centred situation.

So much, then, for what the book is not about. What *are* its scope and intentions? Briefly, to provide a conceptual framework in which comprehensive productivity bargaining can be understood; to summarise the salient features of the experience gained so far, both from agreements which have been successfully concluded and those which have been abortive; to give practical guidance by discussing some of the main problems which arise and by outlining ways in which they can be dealt with. We are predominantly concerned with unit schemes, that is, schemes for natural operating units—for example, in manufacturing industry, a single plant or site (although, obviously, external factors must be taken into account)—and mainly with hourly paid workers.

The question may then arise, to what extent is it possible to say anything useful at the unit level? Many of the specific problems will be unique to the unit, and therefore not susceptible to generalisation. Some of them result from the state of the particular industry or sphere of activity. The problems of the motor industry are different in degree and in kind from those of the electronics industry, and an analysis of the state of any particular industry is outside our scope. The answer is that many such problems arise from a misuse of human resources: from industrial relations systems which are inappropriate, outdated and, as systems, dynamically unstable. In the current widespread acceptance of productivity bargaining may be seen more than a temporary recognition of an economic need, whether on a personal or national basis. It springs from a more permanent desire to reduce conflict and to make life more meaningful and more effective.

We hope and expect that the book will be of most use to those managers and trade unionists who are, or who become, directly engaged in productivity agreements and who share our beliefs that:

1   There is an under-utilisation of our current physical resources of the order of 20–25 per cent.

2   The main reason for this under-utilisation is the failure to use human resources correctly.

3   Optimum utilisation cannot be achieved by a piecemeal approach, but requires comprehensive changes in our industrial relations policies and practices.

4   In spite of some appearances to the contrary, there is a generally favourable climate at unit level in which these changes can be made.

Essentially, the initiative must come from management. Perhaps for the first time, managements now have the opportunity to re-structure situations rather than merely to react to them. This means, of course, that the unions have an opportunity to support them in any genuine attempt they make.

This is not, then, productivity bargaining in the narrow sense of limited one-off agreements. Nor is it meant in the sense of those agreements which conform to only PIB criteria, since there are many industries and services which cannot, in the short term, produce the evidence to satisfy these. We are concerned primarily with the restructuring of industrial relations and suggest that, at this point in time, productivity bargaining is a useful vehicle.

Acknowledgements

This book draws substantially upon the experience gained in the Industrial and Human Relations Division of Associated Industrial Consultants. This Division was set up in 1961 by Ted Fletcher, to whom we owe a great deal of gratitude for our personal as well as professional development.

We acknowledge the contribution made by our colleagues in the Division both for the discussions we have had whilst working together and for their individual efforts in developing and applying new techniques. In particular we would mention Fred Staples, who is responsible for the mathematics of the Direct Consensus Method of job evaluation, for the reapplication of time-saved bonus schemes and in conjunction with John Heath of the use of input-output models. We are grateful for the comments and assistance given in the preparation of the book by Oliver Tynan, Ron Dickens, Bob Park, and John Castle.

The views and opinions expressed in this book, however, are our own and not necessarily representative of AIC or Ted Fletcher or those of our colleagues.

We wish also to record our appreciation to certain client companies for permission to illustrate our ideas with examples from our work with them. In this connection we would mention in particular, Tube Investments Limited and Imperial Metal Industries (Kynoch) Limited. To preserve the confidential nature of our relations with clients, no direct reference to the company concerned is made where such illustrations or examples are given.

Finally we record our thanks to our wives without whom, we sometimes felt, the book would have been completed more quickly— but it is more likely that it would not have been completed at all.

D T B NORTH
G L BUCKINGHAM

Part I

BACKGROUND TO
PRODUCTIVITY BARGAINING

| 1 | Productivity Bargaining in Depth | 1 |
| 2 | Employee Motivation and Industrial Relations | 9 |

One

Productivity Bargaining in Depth

What are productivity bargains? A useful starting point is research paper number 5 of the Royal Commission on Trade Unions and Employers' Associations. The paper distinguishes between *wage bargaining*, which negotiates increases in wages accordingly to criteria such as the cost of living, comparability, or the ability of the industry, plant or section to pay more, and *wage–work bargaining*, in which a definite undertaking is made in exchange for wage increases. It suggests that the latter comprises four possible categories:

1   Negotiations undertaken by employers' associations and unions into which a specific productivity element is injected, for example, one-man operation of buses.

2   Industry-wide agreements which provide a framework for local productivity bargains to be concluded at unit level. Typical examples are those of the rubber and chemical industries. These agreements are the ones which show most promise, which are becoming more prevalent and which form the major consideration in this book.

3   The small-scale negotiations usually associated with the introduction of work study. These are the traditional agreements covering a department or small unit.

4   The so-called "classical" productivity bargains concluded (for example) by Esso Petroleum Company Limited, British Oxygen Company Limited and the former Steel Company of Wales. Because of their influence and the stimulus they provided, these deserve detailed comment.

These agreements were basically an exchange of higher wages for more work or the same wages in less time, or for greater flexibility and mobility of labour. In terms of content, they were not significantly novel. Similar agreements involving wage–work relationships had been made for many years, through piecework or incentive schemes, agreements to changes in work roles and the like. They were, however, characterised by several features which were, if not novel, at least relatively rare and relatively unknown:

1   The positive policies adopted by management, instead of a policy of containment.
2   The style of the negotiations. The real problems and the facts supporting them were laid on the negotiating table, not swept under the carpet. Discussions were on a plant-wide, multi-union basis.
3   The total operational cost reduction was taken into account and not (as was more usual) the reduction in labour costs only. A realistic share of this was offered, instead of an acceptable negotiable increase on current wage levels.

There were, of course, limitations to these earlier agreements. Although plant-wide, they dealt with only certain aspects of the total situation. They were introduced in capital-intensive, low labour cost, process-controlled plants and they were—at any rate ostensibly —one-off agreements. However, they not only achieved their objectives but bore other beneficial results, notably in improving the climate of industrial relations. Because of this and the substantial publicity rightly given them it was not surprising that other managements tried to follow suit—nor that, faced with a need to curb wage increases, the Government through the Prices and Incomes Board first encouraged and then attempted to compel them to do so.

Need for comprehensive approach

These classical agreements were followed by diverse attempts to achieve productivity deals in other industries, with varying degrees of success. In some plants the agreements took the form of the "buying out" of tea breaks—though it should be noted that, apart from machine or process controlled operations, all the research evidence suggests that tea breaks improve productivity. In others, joint

2

consultative or problem-solving committees were set up. There are some successful examples here, notably that of Ilford Limited, the photographic manufacturer: savings resulting from suggestions which are implemented go into a wages pool, from which wage increases are negotiated. There are, however, problems of costing and of agreeing the share. In the main, where this approach was attempted, industrial relations improved but there were insufficient backing services to enable real progress to be made.

Other managements started on a rationalisation of the wages system, with or without the support of the unions. Again, some succeeded but many others eventually found they had a solution which could not be applied because of the cost or was not acceptable because of the anomalies, whilst pressure for wage increases was building up. Yet other attempts to negotiate agreements failed because of union problems: inability to reach agreement with the shop stewards or, having reached agreement with them, rejection of both shop stewards and agreement by the work-force.

What conclusions can be drawn from this experience? All these attempts, whether successful or not and whatever their starting point, came up against the total industrial relations situation in the unit and had to take account of it. Failure to do so meant, at best, a limited one-off agreement leaving a significant potential for increased productivity untapped or, at worst, an increased frustration on all sides, with perhaps decreased productivity. Common sense thus dictates that the starting point for any realistic productivity agreement is an examination of the total work situation, and that a comprehensive analysis to identify the size and shape of the problems is required.

The early chapters of this book are devoted to the methods of identifying the specific problems within the total scene. This involves an analysis of four main areas: production, economic, sociological and earnings. The size and shape of these problems will be unique to the unit, but it is possible to indicate the general problems which are common to most. They can be summarised as follows:

1   The irrelevance of most national industry-wide agreements to pay and productivity problems. The engineering industry, for example, is caught in the strait-jacket of its wages structure. Rationalisation cannot take place without substantial, uneconomic increases at national level, yet there are no real

means of effecting economies other than by individual companies. The sort of productivity increases we are concerned with here (that is, the increased utilisation of current resources) take place at unit level, and this is where bargains should be made.

2   The large number of job categories—craft skills or occupational groupings which result in, or are perhaps caused by, a multi-union structure. These cause problems of inter-union rivalry, of different payment structures and insupportable differentials in payment levels.

3   The failure of previously successful practices to apply in changing social and economic circumstances. However useful the bowler-hatted foreman with the power of the sack, or arbitrary piecework rate fixing systems may once have been, both are ineffective in present day circumstances.

4   The lack of managerial initiative in re-structuring industrial relations; in particular the failure to integrate the role of the work-force and the increasingly important role of the shop steward.

5   The lack of simple coherent remuneration policies. The failure to recognise, on any unit, plant or company basis, the inevitable conflict about the relative shares of the revenue has resulted in payment systems which have neither rhyme, reason nor, in spite of expressed intentions, any positive motivational aspect.

The chapters of the book following the analysis indicate the ways in which these problems can be dealt with and consider the design of an integrated industrial relations system. To complete our summary, however, we must add:

6   The need for more managers to acquire a fuller understanding of the motives of people at work.

For many years managers have, on the whole, consistently ignored not only the results of research into human motivation but also the evidence of their own experience. This has led them to invent elaborate theories to explain why—for example—since people work for money, they do not maximise their earnings under, say, a piecework system. One is continually surprised at the elaborations of these theories as they are assailed more and more by the evidence. They are reminiscent of the Indian philosopher who knew the world was supported on the back of a turtle. "But what is the turtle supported by?" he was asked. "By an elephant." "What then supports the elephant?" "Something, I know not what."

The understanding of motivation, of what makes people give of their best, is in fact the key not only to productivity bargaining and good industrial relations, but to many other problems. Managers achieve their production targets not through their own physical efforts but through those of other people. In view of its importance, the subject of motivation forms the second chapter of this book. The reader will be invited to discard the few simple rules by which we have all tried to cope with the complex situation of people at work, and to substitute a perhaps more esoteric, but also more robust and practical set of concepts.

The reader may have detected a bias towards manufacturing industry, for it is here that more measurement controls exist. Some of the measurement techniques described later are, however, applicable to many situations outside industry. It is our belief that the approach and principles outlined are capable of almost universal application.

What then, in short, is our standpoint? That productivity bargaining can be more than a palliative for an immediate problem; that it can also be much more than is implied by the criteria of the Prices and Incomes Board.

To be successful and continuously effective, a productivity agreement should re-structure the total industrial relations situation in a plant. This demands a careful analysis of all the problems involved; experimentation in devising a new system; courage and confidence in applying it. Only by this comprehensive approach is it possible, through the proper use of human resources, to utilise our physical resources fully.

A substantial part of the book deals with wages, an emphasis which reflects the importance the writers attach to this part of the total system: not because "people only work for money," but because the method of payment is one of the most important ways in which the basic philosophy of a company is expressed. A wages system reinforces a company's values. How a more progressive philosophy can be expressed through a more dynamically stable wages system is explained in our exposition of a "three-tier" system.

What sort of agreement, and hence industrial relations system, are we suggesting? The following gives a preview.

Contents of a comprehensive agreement

Security of employment plan

This will be based upon realistic manpower planning, taking into account the market trends and technological changes involving different skills as well as numbers. It should also take into account the social and demographic factors of the region. It will be expressed as a set of rules which the management will follow, covering measures to avoid redundancy by prediction of needs, recruitment restrictions, retraining, redeployment, periods of warning and notice, dismissal criteria, compensation, assistance in finding other work and appeals. The company is not expected to provide work in perpetuity but to avoid sudden decisions and lessen hardship.

Role specification and measurement

The role specifications for the work-force will be prepared in terms of the unit objectives. These lead to the possibilities of job enlargement, changes in working practices, a basis for a rational graded wages system and a realistic measurement of the roles. This measurement will be in terms not solely of work content, but also of plant utilisation, material yield or quality, as appropriate to the role. The methods of measurement and the standards, together with the procedures for their amendment and periodic review, form part of the agreement.

Rational wages system

The method of payment reinforces a company's values. The main characteristics of a wages system (or salary system) should be that:

1   Earnings should reflect the agreed differentials in job worth. These differentials should be maintained. Between four and nine grades are sufficient for most shop-floor operations.
2   There should be a variable element which reflects the measured performance in the role of the natural operating unit. The variable element should be stabilised, to avoid differences in payment for small differences in performance, and predictable, by payment being fixed over a time period at a rate determined by previous performances.

6

3   There should be a means for increasing earnings as a whole, that is, for lifting the whole structure. A useful device for this which has more theoretical than practical limitations is an annual improvement factor determined by an index of, say, wages to added value.

This index also acts as a focus for discussions about the productivity of the unit as well as introducing an element of economic realism into a wages system.

Communications structure

This structure is what makes the system work. It comprises:

1   *Command system*: the management information flow system which ensures that even the supervisor knows what is going on.
2   *Consultation system*: centred on small unit productivity panels which are fed with information and participate actively in the matters which closely concern them.
3   *Negotiation system*: to deal with areas of inevitable conflict. There should be a multi-union body for the unit, with properly trained representatives enjoying adequate facilities.
4   *Appeals system*: to allow individual grievances to be aired at successive levels of the hierarchy as necessary.

Rules and procedures

These will specify the basic codes of conduct, time keeping and attendance standards, disciplinary procedures, working and shift arrangements and the like.

Fringe benefits

While there are certainly pressures for more equality—for example, with staff in terms of pensions and sickness benefits—there is often no acceptance of these by the work-force as an alternative to increased wages except within a few productivity agreements.

All this must be carried out within the economic environment in which the unit is operating. An assessment of this environment and a realistic estimate of the costs and implications must be obtained.

The concluding chapters are devoted to the problems which productivity agreements pose for management and unions. In the short term, there are the specific problems of implementation; in the longer term, the problems of adapting to a changed climate. The writers' main hope is then that they can make a contribution towards the development of radically improved industrial relations practices which will lead not only to a substantial improvement in the utilisation of physical resources but to more satisfying working lives.

Two

Employee Motivation and Industrial Relations

In the previous chapter, it was suggested that the negotiation of a comprehensive productivity agreement gives management, perhaps for the first time, an opportunity to re-structure its industrial relations in a company or plant. The publicity given to productivity bargaining since the announcement of the Esso agreement at the Fawley refinery, and the subsequent attention it has received, have had a number of effects. Perhaps the most important is the change in attitude to industrial relations which it has created.

Today managers are seeking a theory of employee motivation which, when applied will identify the work-force with the company and obtain its commitment to company objectives. They want employees who are prepared to work towards high performance goals, employees who are willing to be flexible and to accept change as the speed of technological development increases.

Traditional concepts of employee motivation

Until recently some managements were concerned to provide their employees with a working environment and conditions of service that would create a contented, stable labour force, and to develop a range of personnel policies covering fringe benefits and social and welfare amenities. In so doing, they were consciously or unconsciously reflecting the findings of the "benign environment" school of industrial sociology, which believed the provision of good working

9

conditions and secure, comprehensive conditions of employment would improve employees' morale and create high levels of productivity. But experience revealed that the provision of such facilities did not of itself create a high tempo of work or the degree of identification with the company which the managements had hoped for.

Not all companies have developed defined personnel policies based on an explicit view of the motivation of their employees. However, like Molière's Monsieur Jourdain, who had been talking prose for the last forty years without knowing it, companies implicitly reflect their ideas about motivation through their payment systems, employment conditions and attitudes to trade unions even though they are unaware that they are expressing their philosophy.

These basic assumptions about people at work have been analysed by Douglas McGregor in his book *The Human Side of Enterprise*. He shows that the employment policies and practices of the majority of companies reflect a commonly held view about people's motivation in the work situation. This he calls theory X—the traditional view of direction and control. He summarises the assumptions about people on which theory X is based in this way.

First, most people dislike work and avoid it wherever possible. Accordingly, employees have to be coerced, directed and pressures applied to them if they are to make a sufficient effort in their jobs. Second, most people prefer being directed: they avoid responsibility where possible, and above everything else want security. Assumptions of this sort are frequently described by the phrase "carrot and stick" management. In many companies a rigid application of these views has produced a conflict-prone industrial relations situation, and the confrontation between the "two sides" of industry—management and organised labour—is only too apparent.

Changing views of motivation

However, companies with such a philosophy are beginning to question its validity and starting to change. A major British tyre manufacturer, Avon Rubber Company Limited, in advertisements for managerial and other professional staff, announced that it was introducing a theory Y philosophy. This is McGregor's term for what he believes is a more realistic management philosophy which is consistent with current research knowledge, and which better accounts for people's behaviour at work. We shall look briefly at some of the findings of this research later; the point we would emphasise here is that the preparation of a productivity agreement which will have long-term benefits necessitates examination of these basic assumptions about human behaviour and the way in which employees can be encouraged to give of their best.

When entering upon such an exercise, management has to choose the sort of industrial relations it wishes to develop in the company. It must clarify its views about employee motivation, as these will determine both the nature of the agreement and the way in which it is implemented. For example, whilst the importance of wages structures and their rationalisation are emphasised later, as a central factor for many companies in devising an effective productivity agreement, we will attempt to set this in the context of the total motivational framework which the company is seeking to establish.

Since the Second World War, extensive research has been carried out in Britain, Europe and particularly in the United States, into the behaviour of employees in the industrial situation. The work of American behavioural scientists has found a wide audience on both sides of the Atlantic, through the books of Douglas McGregor and Rensis Likert. McGregor and Likert have put forward proposals for a new system of management philosophy or style which, in the latter's case, is supported by the extensive research carried out under the auspices of the Institute for Social Research of the University of Michigan.

Hierarchy of needs

The work of McGregor and Likert stems from the findings of men like Maslow and Herzberg about the nature of employee motivation. Maslow's theory suggests that human needs are organised into a series of different levels—a hierarchy of importance. This is shown diagrammatically in Figure 2:1. The ascending order of importance of this hierarchy is as follows.

Man's *basic* needs are physiological, for example hunger, thirst, sleep and so on. When these are satisfied they are replaced by *safety* needs reflecting his desire for protection against danger or deprivation. These in turn, when satisfied, are replaced by *social* needs, which are functions of man's innate gregariousness and his desire to belong to a group, to give and receive friendship and to associate happily with people. Above this, Maslow affirms there are *egoistic* needs related to our desire for self-esteem and self-respect, which are affected by our standing, reputation and our need for recognition and appreciation. Finally, individuals have a need for self-fulfilment, which is bound up with their views about the purpose of life and is a reflection of their urge for self-development and to be creative in the broadest sense of the word.

```
┌─────────────────────────────────────────────┐
│                                             │
│           SELF—ACTUALISATION                │
│        (Desire for self—fulfilment)         │
│                                             │
├─────────────────────────────────────────────┤
│                                             │
│              ESTEEM NEEDS                   │
│          (Success, self—respect)            │
│                                             │
├─────────────────────────────────────────────┤
│                                             │
│         BELONGINGNESS AND LOVE              │
│         (Affection, identification)         │
│                                             │
├─────────────────────────────────────────────┤
│                                             │
│              SAFETY NEEDS                   │
│            (Security, order)                │
│                                             │
├─────────────────────────────────────────────┤
│                                             │
│          PHYSIOLOGICAL NEEDS                │
│            (Hunger, thirst)                 │
│                                             │
└─────────────────────────────────────────────┘
```

FIGURE 2:1   HIERARCHY OF HUMAN NEEDS

McGregor applies Maslow's theory to the industrial situation and emphasises that man continuously puts forth effort or work in order to satisfy these needs and that, as one need is satisfied, so another appears in its place. The limitation of this theory is, perhaps, that it appears to provide an oversimplified solution to what is really an extremely complex problem. The clear-cut series of levels which Maslow propounds ignores the fact that human desires and aspirations are confused and intermingled, but the theory does provide an extremely important and useful conceptual framework.

It is pertinent to the industrial situation because it suggests that the criteria which managements use as the basis of their views on employee motivation are limited, and the industrial environment is restricted as a result. The criteria are related almost entirely to people's lower-level needs for safety and physiological security, for protection against deprivation and the threat to self or family; they do little, except fortuitously, to satisfy the higher needs of individuals in the employment situation.

Motivation–hygiene theory

An important development of this concept of the "hierarchy of needs" has been propounded by Frederick Herzberg in his "motivation–hygiene" theory of motivation, originally developed as a result of research based on depth interview studies with engineers and accountants. Herzberg differentiates between factors which lead to satisfaction in the industrial situation—"satisfiers"—and those which contribute little to satisfaction but create feelings of frustration and unhappiness—"dissatisfiers." Figure 2:2 compares satisfying and dissatisfying aspects of the employment situation, based on Herzberg's findings. It reveals that the higher level needs of Maslow tend to be those which Herzberg identifies as positive motivating forces, whereas the lower level of needs in Maslow's hierarchy appear to be dissatisfiers to employees when they are not fulfilled although they do not produce positive motivation when they are.

Herzberg points out that these dissatisfying or "hygiene" factors are generally satisfied for only a limited period and continually require replenishing. Financial reward is a prime example of this. Individuals may at any one point in time feel that they are equitably paid, but after a while their expectations increase and they feel dissatisfied unless an increase in earnings is forthcoming.

He stresses the need for managements to turn their attention to the positive motivating factors such as achievement, the work itself and responsibility, and to develop policies of "job enrichment" which will fulfil these requirements. These views have aroused considerable interest, and experiments are being carried out, notably at Imperial Chemical Industries Limited, to test these findings in the industrial situation.

One large American company, Texas Instruments, under the guidance of its personnel research director E Scott Myers, has put these motivational theories into practice over a number of years and can now claim wide experience of their effects. The company has

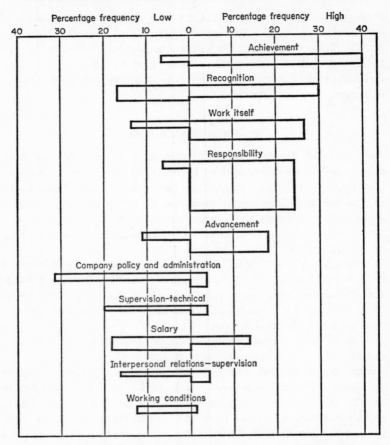

FIGURE 2:2   COMPARISON OF SATISFIERS AND DISSATISFIERS

one of the most rapid growth records in American industry since the war, which is due at least partly to the fact that from its inception it explicitly set out to "grow" managers. The emphasis has been on satisfying employees' basic needs and then, wherever possible, creating a climate which *positively* motivates people in their jobs. This principle is applied right down to the production lines, where the organisation of work emphasises the development of all employees' full range of abilities. Texas Instruments' view is that, while good earnings levels are important, there are other equally important factors, such as the individual's pride in his work and his interest in

14

developing the job. For example, production employees are encouraged to find new methods of doing their task more effectively. Each employee is trained in "work simplification" methods and procedures so that he (or she) can apply simple method study techniques and other tools of logical thinking to improvements appropriate to their own level of activity. In this way, the company focuses employees' attention on increased productivity, the enhanced use of materials and so on, and seeks to create an environment which is challenging and satisfying in that all employees can make a positive and worthwhile contribution to a specified objective during their period of work.

Principle of supportive relationships

It is primarily Rensis Likert who has taken the implication of these findings about employee motivation and from them developed a specific, comprehensive theory of management philosophy and organisation. He propounds a science-based organisational theory founded on the principle of supportive relationships as the crux of effective "man management" in any company. This supportive relationship between superior and subordinate, Likert suggests, should allow the subordinate to develop his capacities to the full yet not impose threats or constraints upon him. As Likert himself says, "the more often the superior's behaviour is ego-building rather than ego-deflating, the better will be the effect of his behaviour on organisational performance."

In developing his thesis on the validity of this principle, which is combined with an emphasis on the use of group decision making and group methods of supervision, Likert also lays heavy emphasis on the need to develop high performance goals for the organisation by means of these relationships. Members of an organisation, he affirms, wish to achieve. Provided that their opportunities for achievement are structured in a constructive way and their lower needs are satisfied in terms of financial, job-security and status requirements, employees will strive to attain satisfaction and feelings of fulfilment by attaining ever-increasing standards of performance. Commitment to such high performance goals, however, cannot be *imposed*, and superiors have to exercise considerable skill in human relations to develop an environment in which high organisational goals are achieved.

Finally, Likert demonstrates that companies which pay attention to encouraging employees to use their abilities as fully as possible obtain higher levels of production and better organisational performance than those which are technique- and method-centred and which use management tools as restrictions or controls in a punitive or negative sense. The latter companies restrict the opportunities for employees to develop to the full and create a constricted working environment. Few companies have applied Likert's philosophy to the management of their human resources nor have they structured an organisation which allows for the full integration of employees' activities through co-operation. An organisation should seek to use the abilities of all its employees and should be structured so that the sum of its employees' efforts is significantly greater than if each were working as an individual. McGregor describes such a philosophy as theory Y, which he contrasts with the traditional managerial philosophy, theory X.

Most companies achieve reasonable results when it comes to co-ordinating their physical resources and the application of technological development, but ignore the potential improvement to be obtained from recognising the power of groups of effectively motivated people to achieve improved standards of performance. That groups of employees have power in the factory or office has become increasingly evident as union membership and influence has grown in a full employment society. Management has interpreted this trend as a threat and has established mechanisms to meet it.

Basic concepts of management–employee relations

As a result of the exploitation of their labour in the nineteenth century, employees banded together and, through association, gradually put pressure on management to improve their treatment, their conditions and their pay. The rapid growth and increasing strength of trade unions led eventually to a complete change in the balance of power, which managements were slow to recognise. As the unions' strength grew, so management was forced into a defensive position, so that British industrial relations are traditionally based on union initiative and management's adoption of a defensive position.

As employees joined together in unions to exert collective strength, so companies combined in federations and associations to protect themselves from the powers exercised by growing and increasingly militant trade unions. The unions made claims for improved pay and working conditions on which employers, after initial rejection, entered into negotiation. Eventually a compromise was reached, with or without the use of sanctions such as strikes, banning overtime or similar practices. Companies became conditioned to a negative, conciliatory role. Evidence of this still survives in companies whose industrial relations function exists only to contain union pressures. For example, the personnel manager of a company in the engineering industry approached all negotiations on the specific assumption that there would be a "failure to agree" which would enable him to freeze the employees' claims in the delaying processes of the industry's national disputes procedure. Companies used to such an essentially negative approach find the negotiation of a productivity agreement difficult because, for the first time, they have to take the initiative over a range of factors designed to re-structure many of the fundamental conditions of employment. They are not used to making such proposals and are uncertain of the communications and negotiating requirements. They are unsure of employees' reactions and lack the means of discovering them. When to this problem is added the need to reconstruct the entire motivational framework which the company has established for its employees, then the pressures on management become acute.

Restructuring the industrial relations situation

The inadequacies of the present industrial relations situation do not arise from any particularly unfortunate characteristics of the British nation. They are due to the way the situation is structured, and this owes much to the fact that this country led the industrial revolution. The early industrialists followed the "protestant ethic": many were called, few were chosen, and the chosen few would attain superiority by their own efforts. It followed that most people were failures and would find no satisfaction in their work. Fear and, where economic conditions required it, bribery were the mainsprings of the entrepreneur's inducements to his work-force.

This attitude was an extreme example of the theory X philosophy. It created the need for workers' organisations, and from it has stemmed the conflict which bedevils industrial relations today. The manager, having largely lost his power, clings tenaciously to the concept of prerogative, even though it has become largely meaningless.

Behaviour patterns revealed in our industrial relations reflect the existing situation and the beliefs of those concerned. Changes in behaviour are needed if the skills and abilities of the working population are to be used more effectively, but these changes can only stem from new beliefs and a revised structure. The research findings described in this chapter throw some light upon people's behaviour at work and suggest the framework of a new, more constructive philosophy.

Part II

CONDUCT OF THE FEASIBILITY STUDY FOR A PRODUCTIVITY AGREEMENT

3	*Scope and Organisational Implications*	21
4	*Production Analysis*	29
5	*Economic Analysis and Costing*	41
6	*Sociological Analysis*	50
7	*Analysis of the Wage System and its Effects*	62

Three

Scope and Organisational Implications

It will be clear from previous chapters that, when discussing a productivity agreement, we are advocating much more than a short-term wage–work bargain or "buy-out" of restrictive practices. Instead we suggest that what can—and should—be developed is a radical re-structuring of the industrial relations situation, and that this requires detailed, comprehensive studies to identify the size and shape of the problems.

Any major changes will be applied within a complex and inter-linked system or series of systems designed to optimise the productive resources of the organisation. Changes in one area will affect many others. For example, a new system of payment will, among other things, affect the roles of management and supervision, employees' attitudes and motivation, the role of shop stewards and their bargaining power, the production control system and the pressures upon it, and so on.

Furthermore, changes will be contemplated in an area where management lacks the power to implement its decisions unilaterally. It must obtain the agreement of the work-force and its representatives. This is sometimes a major problem, particularly where shop stewards are powerful and militant. In the early days of one assignment, for example, the writers were discussing the need for job evaluation with a senior shop steward. He saw little value in the technique. The matter was quite simple: all that was required was three or perhaps four grades into which he would put all the jobs.

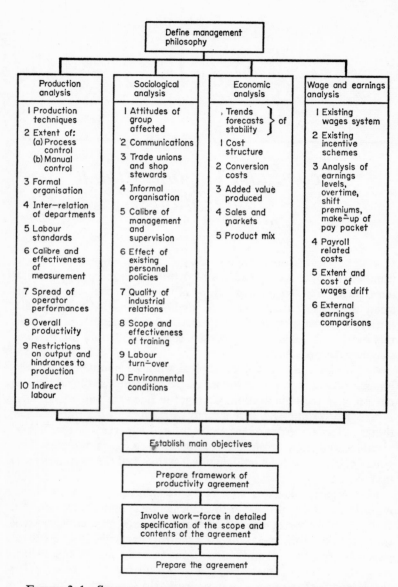

FIGURE 3:1   SCHEMATIC REPRESENTATION OF THE FEASIBILITY STUDY

When asked what would happen if either of us, as one of his members, queried his decision about the grading of our job, the reply revealed his degree of control of the situation. "You don't work here, mate."

This shop steward was particularly well established. In the middle of the plant was a little hut, to which he retired on any afternoon when not engaged in negotiations. A steady stream of visitors called to see him, bringing complaints and queries. He obtained a regular flow of information about the earnings levels of his members (the company concerned operated a range of different payment-by-results systems, many of which were loose). Every so often he would sally forth from his retreat to submit to management a new claim, based on the evidence he accumulated each day.

Where the power of a particular shop steward has grown to this extent, a range of factors will have contributed to the situation. If a company wishes to do anything about it, these factors and their influence on relationships must be identified and explored. Because this area is complex, it means that economically there may be a high risk element. Ill conceived proposals which have not been thoroughly examined and carefully worked out can have a serious effect upon the company's manufacturing costs and performance, and could seriously affect its profitability.

A detailed feasibility study therefore needs to be carried out when a comprehensive productivity agreement is contemplated. The main elements in such a study are the production, sociological, economic and wages and earnings analyses (shown diagrammatically in Figure 3:1). In the following four chapters we shall be discussing what is involved in analysing the existing company situation under each of these elements. But before such studies are carried out, management has to take a fundamental decision: what size of organisational unit will the investigation cover?

Area of investigation

Company, plant, or department?

This initial decision is extremely important. Are changes to be made on a company, factory, departmental, or sectional basis? Clearly, the answer to such a question depends on a wide range of factors, and no universal reply is possible. There is, however, a national trend which is particularly significant for large- and medium-sized companies, and which is the basis of our approach to this subject. This trend, observable in many industries, is the growing importance of plant or factory negotiations at the expense of industry-wide, nationally negotiated agreements. Increasingly, agreements negotiated on an industry-wide basis at national level are providing for, or encouraging, factory or plant productivity agreements (for example, in the chemical and rubber industries). These pressures tend to establish the area of investigation as the individual plant or factory. [See, for example, the recommendations on this matter by the report of the Royal Commission on Trade Unions and Employers' Associations (the Donovan report).]

This tendency is increased by the problems encountered with traditional payment-by-results schemes. Commonly, these have been introduced on an *ad hoc* basis over long periods of time in different departments and sections. The longer a scheme has been in operation, the more likely it is that standards have become slack. Furthermore, the accuracy of standards may vary on account of differing processes, the degree of militancy among shop stewards and employees, or varying work study expertise. These and other factors lead to wide variations in earnings levels for jobs of similar worth and equal employee performance across departments. Frequently the department or section with the lowest standard of performance has the greatest degree of wage drift and therefore, in many cases, the highest earnings levels. Equity, cost considerations and improved management control, to say nothing of negotiating realities, all point to the need to rationalise above and beyond departmental or sectional levels—that is, across the plant or factory.

The importance of deciding whether the agreement is to be single or multi-plant may be illustrated from recent experience. A company embarked on a comprehensive productivity bargaining programme in each of its three factories. These were separated from each other by some six to nine miles, and at the outset the company laid down that one objective of the exercise was to establish uniform earnings levels for similar jobs. It proposed, in fact, to establish a uniform company wage structure with identical earnings levels.

Although the factories were geographically close and, in the case of the two larger factories, technologically identical, the calibre, attitude and performance of their employees varied substantially. So also did the degree of union membership, the climate of industrial relations and the militancy of employees and shop stewards. Finally, there were clear differences in the market rates of the areas concerned, while the lower paid and lower performance plant was next door to other plants of the group.

When the facts of the situation were exposed, the costs of a policy of uniform payment became apparent. In brief, it would have required the higher paid and more militant plants to subsidise the lower paid and less militant one. Had this policy been implemented, it would have created real problems for the factories of the group on the same site. And it would have meant that the agreement would have been an uneconomic proposition, involving a great deal of effort, trouble and expense for little or no reduction in unit labour costs.

So the decision was changed. Each plant negotiated its own agreement, setting its own levels of earnings in relation to the potential increases in productivity, current market rates, the distribution of earnings within each plant, and so on. Within each plant, on the other hand, differences in pay between departments were adjusted so that a uniform system of differentials on a plant basis was established.

Problem of the large company

The desirability of developing agreements on a plant or factory basis, relating earnings to the local market situation, suggests an approach to a related problem which many large companies are currently facing. These are the companies which have, over the last decade, decentralised their organisation, devolving responsibility to product divisions and establishing close profitability criteria as performance yardsticks. Divisional managements are often given considerable autonomy to take decisions and to initiate and implement policies within limits prescribed by company policy.

This type of structure frequently poses problems in the development of industrial relations policies, particularly on multi-divisional sites. These problems commonly centre on the means of providing autonomous divisions with professional "staff" expertise, and the degree to which managerial authority must be prescribed in the interests of overall company requirements. Industrial relations is the aspect of the company's affairs which most frequently calls for modification of the policy of complete decentralisation. The trade unions take little account of the structure of a company and exert pressures in two ways:

1   By pressing for the most attractive wage and employment conditions existing in any division to be applied to all divisions.

2   By "leap-frogging" wage claims or other demands between autonomous divisions. This is particularly liable to happen to a company which has a large number of divisions on the same geographical site, although in some large companies, unions exert such pressures on a regional and even national basis.

Thus decentralisation can present trade unions with excellent opportunities to exert continual pressure for increases in wage rates, earnings levels and other conditions of employment, so making managerial control difficult.

A decentralised organisational structure has even more profound effects upon the way in which a company's industrial relations climate develops. Divisional managers are frequently under continual pressure to meet or exceed their divisional targets. These are frequently established and reviewed on an annual or biannual basis—a relatively short time-scale. Furthermore, management in such an organisation is sometimes paid largely on the basis of its performance against the standards. Both these factors influence managers into taking short-term decisions when confronted by the power of their employees or by difficult market situations. Such action frequently takes the form of concessions to employee pressures for enhanced earnings through, for example, the loosening of standard times or even short-term redundancies because of a temporarily difficult order situation. The former creates pressures on other parts of the company in the same district as well as permanently increasing labour costs; the latter makes employees feel insecure, hardens their attitudes to the company and creates a most unfavourable image of it as an employer.

Creation of an industrial relations policy

For these reasons, it is frequently necessary to limit the autonomy of divisional managers in the area of industrial relations. This requires the creation of defined company industrial relations and personnel policies, and the establishment of an effective personnel department which can interpret these policies to line management and assist in ensuring that they are implemented. We shall comment on the role of the personnel function in Chapter 16. In the present context, it must be asked, on what basis should company-wide industrial relations policies be established? The following principles are suggested as a framework:

1   The most important resources of a company are its employees. Their attitudes, expectations and motivation are a primary concern of management.

2   Management must not seek short-term savings at the expense of employee's motivation and morale. When morale declines, the company incurs long-term costs in matters such as increased labour turnover, resistance to change, the development of restrictive practices and lower productivity which may take years to rectify.

3   It is management's responsibility to take the initiative in industrial relations, wherever possible on a problem-solving basis with well-organised trade unions. A well-developed and effectively manned personnel function can provide significant assistance in this policy of initiation, provided it is not overloaded with "fire-fighting" responsibilities that preclude it carrying out a more constructive role.

4   In large companies with a decentralised organisation structure, some limitation of divisional autonomy is necessary in the interests of control, consistency and overall company development in each district. But it must not become a rigid imposition of centralised personnel policies. Large companies with plants scattered around the country should negotiate group, regional, or plant productivity agreements within a defined company-wide framework. This framework should be sufficiently flexible to give local managements scope for initiation in relation to company needs and enable them to establish policies, particularly in regard to levels of remuneration which are compatible with market rates in the locality.

In our view, therefore, the majority of effective productivity agreements which have been, and will continue to be, negotiated in the context of the current industrial relations framework will be at plant or factory level. These agreements will be effective only if they are based upon detailed analysis of the existing industrial relations and productivity situation in the plant. This needs to be established, and the feasibility of any proposed changes validated, by a detailed and comprehensive study.

Such analysis is described in some detail in subsequent chapters and we shall comment more fully on the implications for management of assessing the current situation and then developing and implementing a comprehensive agreement. At this stage, one point should be emphasised. A team from the production, personnel, industrial engineering and accounting functions is required for such an exercise. For some at least this will be a full time project. In addition, outside assistance is likely to be needed if the necessary objectivity is to be achieved and if a change in the basic relations between management and work-force is to be successfully engineered through a productivity bargain in depth. The minimum number for this team to make any real headway is four, on a full-time basis, and they should expect to spend between three and six months on the study of the situation.

Four

Production Analysis

Determining the current level of productivity and the scope for improving it is one of the main factors in a productivity agreement. It is also one of the most difficult to analyse.

The early productivity agreements concentrated upon the removal of restrictive practices. To avoid emotive overtones, we prefer to call these "hindrances to production due to the organisation of the work." In Appendix 1 are listed the hindrances which are typically met with. It is our normal procedure to hand this list to supervisors and managers for them to indicate each item's relative degree of importance. It is also our normal procedure to include a blank page for them to record the ones we have not yet heard about! A careful examination of the reasons for the apparent hindrances is required, and a realistic proposal to remove the causes is necessary before successful negotiations can be concluded. It may be that the reason for refusal to transfer from one section to another, even temporarily, is a potential loss of pay. More powerful restrictions (for example, the refusal of some trade unions to allow work study examinations) are symptomatic of the power situation and radical changes are needed before they can be removed. Many so-called restrictive practices are an attempt to safeguard job security. If this basic condition is really tackled, many hindrances can be acceptably removed. The writers are very much opposed to the "buying out" of restrictive practices for their own sake. The real effects, if any, should be accurately costed in realistic productivity terms.

It is convenient to consider the analysis of production initially under two main heads: (*a*) *what to measure?* and (*b*) *how to measure?*

and then to assess the effects and implications—for example, of current and optimum performance levels upon the total unit situation —as part of the analysis.

What to measure

The conventional view is that the measure to be used for the work-force is work content; that what employers pay wages for is man-power. Work study and work measurement techniques have been developed and used extensively for this purpose.

A substantial expansion in the use of work study is now taking place, notably in the electricity boards, in local authorities and on the railways. The Prices and Incomes Board loses no opportunity of encouraging the introduction or more extensive application of work study to the situations that are brought to its attention. Yet still, in 1969, the tasks of only about one third of the working population are measured.

We would, however, question the traditional view (which the Prices and Incomes Board may or may not hold) that work content is the only, or at any rate the only appropriate, measure of work-force activity. It is interesting to note that even in the engineering industry, where work study—and in particular work measurement—have been most extensively applied, it is unusual to find that more than sixty per cent of the tasks have direct standards in any plant. This is due partly to the current limitations of the techniques but also to the irrelevance of work content, especially as a sole measure of the task being performed.

The point we are making, however, has no meaning unless there are better alternatives to work content as a measure of the activity. What then are the alternatives? We must first ask, what is the activity? That is to say, first, what is the main purpose, in terms of the unit objectives, of the task under review? Second, what are the charac-teristics of the role the employee is required to fulfil? It is only by a careful analysis leading to an accurate definition that the most appropriate measure or measures may be identified.

A few simple examples might illustrate the point. Taking the case of a maintenance fitter, the overall cost of operations is reduced if he is doing nothing, that is to say, if all the machines are running. The important measure of his activity is machine activity, and the standard that of minimum down-time. It might be argued that this is to take too simple a view of the situation; that one of the factors influencing down-time is correct routine maintenance, and this is susceptible to measurement in terms of work content. But this is to combine two roles and perhaps strike a balance between the two in terms of costs. The costs taken into account should be more than labour costs.

Without attempting to provide a universal solution to the problem of maintenance, we would suggest that the important measurement factors are the number and frequency of breakdowns and the number of men required to service any one of them. The optimum cost is determined by the machine idle costs and number of men for different levels of service. One of the appropriate techniques here is queuing theory. This approach would determine the complement for break-down maintenance and provide an effective measure of performance in real terms.

A perhaps less controversial illustration is that of a process worker in a chemical plant which is not fully automated. He is required primarily to make occasional adjustments, and can be regarded perhaps as part of the process. Obviously, the work content aspect of turning a wheel or pressing a button is irrelevant. What effect, then, does he have? Can it be expressed in terms of quality? To what extent does his role interact with that of others? Is it the total output with a quality factor built in which measures this activity, that is, by its effects? Passing outside the sphere of manufacturing activity, what are the roles and what are the characteristics surrounding them, of say a shop assistant in a supermarket or a fashion store? Instead of attempting to answer these questions here, we will summarise the requirements for an analysis of work activity in question form.

1 What is the main purpose of the activity in terms of the unit objectives? Is it machine or plant utilisation, material yield, adherence to production or dispatch schedules, quality?

2 What influence can the job holders exert on the operation, and how is this affected? What variability can they introduce into the operation and what degree of control have they?

3 What is the relationship between this operation and other parts of the process?

If we appear to be elaborating a relatively simple concept unnecessarily, it should be pointed out, first, that this kind of analysis is rarely carried out (it is only slightly less rare to find that the objectives of the unit as a whole have been correctly diagnosed); second, that we have frequently met situations where wrong measures were being used—for example, machinists removing defects from material at £3000 per ton were encouraged by an output measure to take a deeper cut to save time, instead of a shallow cut to save material. Third, and most important in view of the large numbers of unmeasured activities, this approach enables a much wider range of measurement techniques to be used, and these are discussed below.

How to measure

The identification of what one is seeking to measure is an important first step in the quantitative analysis. It is to be hoped that what have been identified are the essentials of the activity as well as the system of which the activity forms a part. Is it meaningful to isolate an individual work station? What are the advantages of this in terms perhaps of applying individual measurement, against the disadvantages of providing buffer stocks for the work station, or making allowances for production breakdowns and lack of mobility?

Within the context of a productivity bargain there are two main requirements of measurement. The first is that of obtaining relatively quickly, a reasonable estimate of the activity level and of the restraints upon it. The second is determining targets which can be accepted as achievable, which are robust in relation to the variability of the situation, and which can act as a reference point for the calculation of savings, increase in earnings and managerial control purposes. The conventional, and most reliable, method is to select from records a previous period which was in all essential respects typical of the performances being achieved in terms of the factors being measured. Stage two is the determination of the targets or standards which are expected as a result of the studies. Cost comparisons can then be made in terms of unit costs, increases in yield and the like. This method has three important requirements:

1   That the appropriate records are available and reliable.
2   That there is no time restraint—that is, that the estimate of the effects can wait until accurate standards are available.
3   That there is some objective and absolute (in all except philosophical terms) standard which can be applied. Conventionally, this would be standard performance, rated at 100 per cent on the BS 3138 scale for work content measure.

As regards (1), the records appropriate to the measure being used are either available or not. If not, then adequate procedures must be installed to collect the data, and the bias that may arise through recording during the investigation must be accepted.

For (2) it is usually desirable at an early stage to have some idea, within reasonable tolerances, of the potential. Indeed if the feasibility study is to have much meaning, it is vital that the potential for increase in productivity is used as a factor for determining the overall possibility of the bargain—the problems of absorption by increased sales, reduction in working hours or numbers employed, etc. Later in this chapter the technique of activity sampling is outlined. It is reasonably reliable, and can be carried out in a relatively short space of time.

Item (3) cannot be dealt with so easily and it is worth exploring the problem in some depth. Confronted with any phenomenon, one can organise it according to a conceptual system as follows:

1   "This thing is different from the other." This is a vague judgement perhaps based on some kind of feeling such as instinct or intuition. There is only differentiation at large.

2   "This thing is taller than (greener than, etc) the other." Here a particular attribute has been identified which differentiates the phenomenon from another in a certain way. The attribute permits a method of comparison, provided that it can be distinguished practically and that the distinction can be communicated.

3   "This thing is x centimetres long and has a frequency of y units." In other words, the phenomenon can be identified as a system which conforms to certain mathematical constructs. Once the conformity is identified, the construct can be used to describe in more detail and to make predictions. We leave aside the questions as to whether this is objective or not or whether the standards are absolute.

The main point is that this is a hierarchical system (the third category is more useful than the second but the second is useful to some extent) and it is more useful to have relative standards which enable comparisons of productivity (that is, according to an input to output ratio) than not to differentiate at all.

The progression is usually also in time and, since there are, as we have said, large areas of activity still unmeasured, we suggest that relative standards can and should be used. An example will illustrate the point. In the course of investigating the problems of manual workers in local authorities and hospitals, the Prices and Incomes Board found that the lower grade workers' wage levels were below the minimum acceptable. In order to raise them in a time of wage "freeze," and to conform with criteria of productivity rather than comparability, some measure of productivity increase was desirable. The Board was advised that work study should be introduced, but in view of the size of the problem, it was realised that this would take years to become effective. The writers, asked if they had any proposals, suggested that it might be possible to obtain a measure of current activities on different identifiable units by means of multiple regression analysis (a statistical technique described later in this chapter). Full details of the shorter term scheme are contained in report number 29 of the Prices and Incomes Board, but, in brief, the method was to determine the important variables in the system—the number of dustbins per square mile, lengths of journeys, etc, and to relate them to wage costs by statistical analysis and then determine the degree of consistency. The resulting formula could then be used for comparison with other similar authorities and also as a reference point. Thus improvements in productivity as measured by the formula would allow increased payments to be made. The proposal was tested and found to be practical in spite of considerable doubts and many theoretical objections. However, the suggestion that the ratio and the means of improving it should be used as a focal point in discussions between management and work-force, through local productivity panels, has not been adopted.

It would be interesting, if not particularly relevant, to discuss into which category—relative or absolute—work measurement standards could be placed. Protagonists of work measurement—especially supporters of PMTS—would no doubt claim that their standards are objective and absolute. On one hand, there is plenty of evidence from well conducted experiments that work standards can vary considerably, according to the observer setting them, and, on the other, even more evidence that in many plants and operational activities, standards have been evolved which are verifiable, acceptable and useful.

Work study, and particularly work measurement, systems are useful under the right circumstances as a means of determining current productivity levels and identifying potential improvements.

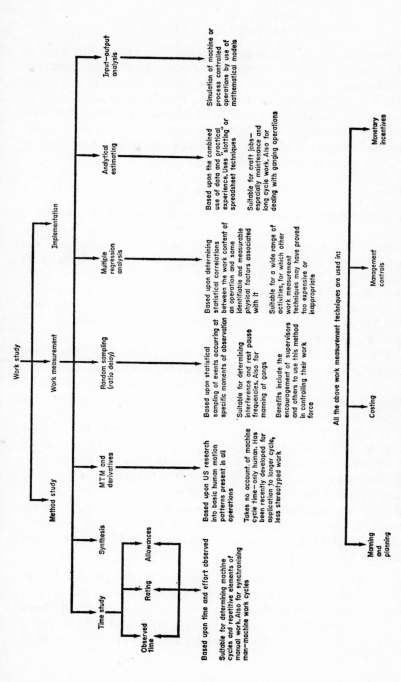

FIGURE 4:1 MEASUREMENT TECHNIQUES SHOWN DIAGRAMMATICALLY

The techniques will not be described here, though it is worth noting that there has been a considerable development of predetermined motion-time systems—for example MTM. [See *Teach Yourself MTM 2*, P M Steele.] These are now able to cover a wider range of activities and they have many advantages over conventional work measurement. What other techniques can be used? The more important ones are briefly described below. The various techniques of measurement are shown in Figure 4:1.

Activity sampling

This technique depends upon the assumption that if a sufficient number of random observations of an activity are made, the characteristics of the sample closely resemble the characteristics of the activity itself. [See: Ralph M Barnes, *Work Sampling*, 1956, W C Brown & Co (USA); and W J Richardson and R Heiland, *Work Sampling*, 1957, McGraw-Hill.] Thus if the number of observations of machines idle during the sample was 10 per cent of the total number of observations, then it could be assumed that the idle machine time was 10 per cent.

The technique allows finer differentiation than this, for example several categories of machine idle, breakdown, shortage of material, etc. The more usual application of activity sampling is to make observations over an extended period, perhaps several months. Apart from the question of time, however, this raises problems of data collection of output and reliability of records. The writers' normal procedure is to carry out an intensive coverage over all the plant for a period of two to three weeks, and to record output accurately at appropriate points. The task force for this obviously depends upon the size of the unit and such things as whether there is shift working, but typically between six and ten observers are required. The sampling activity is followed by further investigation of the main problems revealed—work flow, breakdown, etc. The method has two main drawbacks:

1   The strain imposed on the observers. This is perhaps a small price to pay for the amount of information obtained.

2   There is no *qualitative* assessment. The observation shows whether the man is working or not, whether the machine is working or not; but it does not usually show how effectively they work.

36

So far as the man is concerned, the activities can be rated as part of the observations, and his performance assessed in relation to standard performance. Machine speeds can be recorded too, but they are not so readily rated in most cases.

Effect of machine speeds on productivity

One of the most surprising facts in an investigation into production levels is the lack of information about machine or plant speeds. There are, of course, makers' specifications for many standard machine tools and for other items of plant. Even in these cases, however, quite arbitrary variations are often introduced in working the various materials. Many items of plant and equipment have no maker's specification, having been adapted or built for a special purpose. Usually, speeds are negotiated with the operators according to difficulties encountered in the running-in period. It is rare to find accurate and controlled experiments, the preparation of test pieces, or a thorough examination of the causes of slow running in particular instances. Examples from recent experience are illustrative.

Example 1

At one factory, in order to produce an overdue order on time, members of the production staff worked over a weekend. They operated the plant, without difficulty or detriment, *half as fast again* as the accepted standard.

Example 2

In checking speeds against output, it was found in another case that the tachometers used to indicate machine speed were hopelessly inaccurate. An increase of 12 per cent was obtained by using more accurate instruments.

Example 3

The speed at which a tube mill operated was supposed to be determined by tube diameter, wall thickness and several other variables. A statistical exercise was carried out to discover the relative importance of these factors. There was an apparent variability of approximately ± 15 per cent. This did not account for a variability in operating speeds of 90 per cent, and the variation was eventually explained by correlating the speeds against the amount of work available: the less work available, the slower the speed. By examination of what had been done at peak times in the past, much higher standard speeds were determined.

We have already expressed the view that better utilisation of the nation's existing resources would increase them by 20–25 per cent. In our opinion, some 15 per cent of this could be obtained by operating machines and plant at correct speeds. Hence this is a fruitful area for productivity investigation and merits a good deal more attention than it is receiving at present.

Multiple regression analysis in the measurement of work activities

Multiple regression analysis is a well established statistical technique with many applications in the measurement of work activities. A detailed description is given in Appendix 2, and it is sufficient here to state the broad outlines. In most systems, there are a number of factors which interact with each other. Rarely is there a simple relationship between one factor and another. This is true of many work situations; for example, output varies according to product mix. If the major factors can be identified by knowledge of the activity, or even by insight, the regression analysis can determine the relative weights of the factors. There is a standard computer programme for this, and hence the calculation presents no difficulties. (The programme will also test the significance of the factors initially selected.) The following examples show the variety of activities for which it can be used.

Example 1

A dispatch warehouse handling items ranging from small packets to large crates, with the work-force combining into teams of different sizes according to the work to be done at any one time. The formula relates the main categories of work to man-hours and calculates the performance of the warehouse whatever the variation in types of items handled week by week.

Example 2

A sales office handling inquiries ranging from "Please, what do you make?" to "We are designing a new machine and require components conforming to the following specification. . . ." The time range on any one item was 2–54 minutes, including technical discussions. Obviously, no single inquiry was dealt with on its own and there was considerable interaction between them. A multiple regression analysis formula was used to measure the departmental activity.

The technique was also used in two other examples already quoted, the shorter-term scheme for local authorites and the tube mill. Of course, the standards obtained are relative ones but, provided this is acceptable and that it is taken into account in the application, multiple regression analysis can be used in many situations which are not susceptible to other forms of measurement.

Other measures

In many activities, the work itself cannot be measured and its effects are obscured by other factors. Indirect measures are therefore necessary, and they may take the form of relating the effectiveness (say) of a supervisor to the performance of those supervised. There is, however, one other type of measure, more usually associated with managerial performance, and that is the financial ratio. The uses of such ratios are considered in Chapter 9, but it is worth mentioning here that financial ratios can give useful indexes of group performance. One particularly useful set of indexes can be obtained from the concept of *added value*.

Added value is calculated by deducting the cost of materials and bought-out parts from revenue. It is an important index of the performance of the unit as a whole, and is used in some countries for taxation purposes. Ways in which it can be used as an integral part of the wages system are suggested later. For an explanation of its use as an index, the reader is referred to the article by Professor R J Ball in *Business ratios*, August 1968. On only two or three occasions have the writers found added value to be unreliable, and then it was mainly due to accounting problems such as recent changes in the structure of the accounts or radical changes in the trading characteristics of the company.

Financial ratios can also be used where one of the measures required is material utilisation or yield. Here the calculation should take into account the various categories of scrap—whether process scrap (for example, scaling) or specification scrap, which may be reduced by value analysis—as well as errors. Experience shows that there is a potential saving of at least 5 per cent to be made on material usage in many units, and this is usually a substantial part of total costs.

We have indicated the need to determine precisely what is to be measured and outlined some techniques which can be used for this measurement. Information is therefore available about current performance and potential increases. The effects and implications of the latter must then be assessed in conjunction with the economic analysis.

Five

Economic Analysis and Costing

Increases in productivity, even of the order of 20–25 per cent which we are postulating, have a profound effect upon the unit and not least upon its economics. There is more to be considered than the simple balance sheet of reduction of labour costs on the one hand, increases in earnings on the other. Can the increased output be sold, perhaps at somewhat reduced prices? If not, what problems does this pose? When the productivity agreement is comprehensive, as we are advocating, the economic analysis must also be comprehensive.

Fortunately, however deficient a unit may be in the specialist services required for productivity bargaining, it does not usually lack an accountant. Hence we do not intend here to explain accountancy techniques in detail, but only to indicate the kind of information required and its use. The amount and reliability of the information available will, of course, depend upon the degree of sophistication of the unit. Whatever this sophistication, it is usually highly advisable to have an accountant as at least a part-time member of the investigating team. The initial analysis will cover three broad areas:

1   Economic operating characteristics of the unit.
2   Sales and market trends.
3   Costing.

Economic characteristics of the company

Overall, the economic characteristics of the company can often be expressed most simply in the form of a break-even chart, especially where more sophisticated techniques such as marginal costing are

41

not used. It should be recognised that break-even charts are an over-simplification, and that they rest on such assumptions as:

1   Constant fixed expenses.
2   Constant sales.
3   Constant variable cost structure.
4   All costs are either variable or fixed.
5   Production value within a reasonable range can be expanded or contracted by small increments.

Within these limitations, break-even charts can be useful in high-lighting the effects on profits of changes in major elements of cost. In particular, they can be used to calculate approximately the individual or combined effects on profits of changes in labour cost, productivity, material utilisation, capacity utilisation, sales volume, sales prices, etc.

Three break-even charts prepared from the data in Figure 5:1 are shown in Figure 5:2 (*a*, *b*, *c*). They exhibit different cost structure characteristics:

Chart 5 (*a*): high proportion of labour costs.
Chart 5 (*b*): high proportion of fixed costs.
Chart 5 (*c*): high proportion of material costs.

The effect on profits of changes in the various components of cost have also been calculated. *Some* of the implications of these examples are as follows:

1   In example (*a*), a 5 per cent increase in labour costs would halve the profit at the present level of turnover. A 10 per cent increase in productivity would bring additional profits equal to 17 per cent of labour cost.
2   In example (*b*), a 10 per cent increase in sales volume would increase profits by 110 per cent. A 10 per cent increase in productivity would bring additional profits equal to 26 per cent of labour cost.
3   In example (*c*), a 5 per cent decrease in material costs would increase profits by 55 per cent.

In every case the firms are operating above the break-even point but, although total costs and profits are the same, the break-even points vary:

42

Example (*a*): 84 per cent of present value.
Example (*b*): 90 per cent of present value.
Example (*c*): 83 per cent of present value.

Break-even point may be calculated by the formula:

$$1 - \cfrac{\text{Fixed cost}}{\cfrac{\text{Variable cost}}{\text{Sales}}}$$

		(a)	(b)	(c)
	Fixed costs	£300 000	£500 000	£250 000
	Variable costs: materials	£250 000	£200 000	£550 000
	labour	£500 000	£350 000	£250 000
	Total costs	£1 050 000	£1 050 000	£1 050 000
	Sales	£1 100 000	£1 100 000	£1 100 000
	Profit	£50 000	£50 000	£50 000
	Break—even	£940 000	£1 100 000	£1 920 000
1	Variable costs as a percentage of sales value (i.e. marginal costs)	68·2%	50·0%	72·8%
2	Marginal profit on additional turnover	31·8%	50·0%	27·2%
3	Effect on profit (in £ and %) of:			
(a)	10% increase in sales value	£35 000 70%	£55 000 110%	£30 000 60%
(b)	5% increase/decrease in labour costs	±£25 000 ±50%	±£17 500 ±35%	±£12 500 ±25%
(c)	5% increase/decrease in retail costs	±£12 500 ±25%	±£10 000 ±20%	±£27 500 ±55%
(d)	5% increase/decrease in selling prices	±£55 000 ±110%	±£55 000 ±110%	±£55 000 ±110%
(e)	10% increase in productivity (assuming sold)	£85 000 170%	£90 000 180%	£55 000 110%
4	Increase in profits, by 10% increase in productivity expressed as a percentage of labour cost	17%	26%	22%

FIGURE 5:1 EXAMPLES OF BREAK-EVEN CHARTS AND COST AND PROFIT CALCULATION FOR THREE COMPANIES

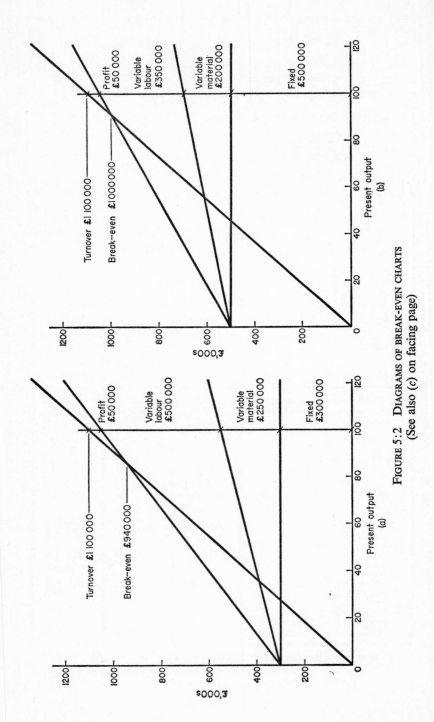

FIGURE 5:2 DIAGRAMS OF BREAK-EVEN CHARTS
(See also (c) on facing page)

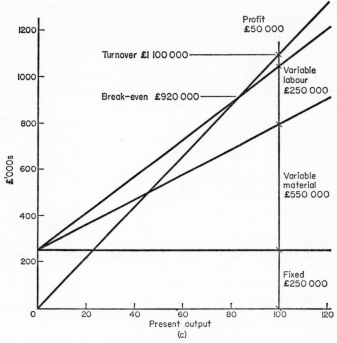

FIGURE 5:2—*continued*

The limitations of break-even points have already been mentioned. They do, however, present a useful total view, and can be used in conjunction with other indicators—for example, added value.

Sales and market trends

One of the scarcest managerial talents is the ability to identify and interpret trends. The common tendency is to wait for something to happen before doing anything about it. This failure of prediction invariably hits the work-force. In times of shrinking order books, some are declared redundant, while in times of rising sales they are expected to work overtime. There are, however, trend effects which are not so easily seen, such as the changes in skills required by advancing technology, or radical shifts in markets requiring greater flexibility of labour, both within a unit and between units. In the context of a comprehensive productivity bargain, there are two important questions in the sales area:

45

1   How much of the projected increased productivity can be absorbed by increased sales?
2   What degree of security of employment can be offered in the light of market trends?

The first question is essentially short term and requires a realistic examination of the present state of affairs for each product or production process.

The second is longer term, and requires prediction not only of the total size of the market for the unit but of its characteristics. Listed below are the most important questions to be asked:

1   Is the market growing or declining? Are there wide fluctuations in market demand?
2   Is there a wide variety of products?
3   Are there frequent changes in the product lines, and a high rate of innovation?
4   Is the market (and the company's share) vulnerable to home or overseas government action?
5   Is technological change likely to affect manufacturing methods significantly?

Sensible answers, quantified wherever possible, are needed to estimate the longer-term implications for manpower planning. In the shorter term, they are used to indicate any likely reductions required in the work-force, and for costing the effects of increased productivity.

Calculation of labour costs

Productivity has been described as a ratio of input to output. The financial implications of a productivity agreement are obtained when one of the factors in the ratio is labour cost and this is related to the change in the ratio due to the agreement. In simple or straightforward situations, of course, the other part of the ratio is the unit of output, and increases in earnings can be compared against increases in productivity. A useful formula for calculating the reduction of labour cost at target performance for target earnings is:

Percentage reduction in labour unit cost =

$$\frac{\text{Percentage increase in productivity} - \text{percentage increase in earnings}}{1 + \text{percentage increase in productivity}}$$

Rarely is the costing of an agreement quite so simple as this. We have mentioned in connection with break-even charts the possible effects on the economies of the unit as a whole. What then, are the problems which are likely to arise in costing an agreement?

In Chapter 11 the problems of rationalising a wages system are described in detail. It is useful here to indicate the major factors to be taken into account. In the first place, there will usually be several costs arising from the restructuring of the system itself. They will include:

1   The increases arising from taking individuals who are currently below it up to the minimum earnings levels, that is, up to the new basic rate or minimum earnings level if the two are different. These individuals will obviously be the lower paid workers, and they will also normally be "indirect" rather than "direct" workers.

2   In most rationalisations the basic rates are substantially increased—for example, in order to make them a more realistic proportion of the total earnings and to take some of the pressure off the incentive system. There may be costs associated with this, for example, on overtime premiums and holiday pay, unless a separate rate is established purely for calculation of such costs. The writers do not favour the establishment of such a rate, and it is also strongly resisted by the unions. A realistic assessment of likely overtime should be made whence total earnings comparisons can be made.

3   The increases in total earnings levels. This is the substance of the bargain. What is being offered for what productivity increase? The cost here depends upon the type of scheme being introduced. It is usually dependent upon the different slopes of the present and proposed bonus curves. The calculation can, of course, be made reasonably easily for target earnings and target performance, but supposing these are not achieved? A calculation is required to enable the risk factors to be taken into account at different intermediate levels of performance. It is worth noting that this problem does not arise with some schemes for sharing time saved.

4   The costs arising from any buying out of anomalous situations. If a protection of earnings system is used, these costs are, strictly speaking, *not* additional costs, since the money

is currently being paid. They do, however, represent a cost against savings resulting from the new system. They represent a real addition when a "buying out" system is adopted.

There are three other potential causes of the increased cost side of the equation. These are the costs associated with:

1   Redundancy payments, especially where it is decided to encourage voluntary redundancy by *ex gratia* payments.
2   Payments for fringe benefits, improved sick pay and pension schemes, etc.
3   Increases to other personnel not necessarily falling within the scope of the agreement—foremen, works staff, etc.

We leave aside the more nebulous costs arising, for example, from payments to worker representatives on productivity panels and the like. These are in the main likely to be small and more than offset by the elimination of incalculable losses due to continual disputes about piece rates and the like. Reduction in labour costs can arise from the following causes:

1   Increases in the rate of working.
2   Elimination of wasted time, perhaps because of an improved work flow system.
3   Improved methods of working, machine utilisation, etc.
4   Improved manning standards.

In the longer term perhaps the most significant benefits will be obtained by achieving control over the wages system—for example, by containing drift, which has been running at the order of 4 per cent a year for at least fifteen years. Too narrow a view should invite Oscar Wilde's criticism of the cynic as one who "knows the price of everything and the value of nothing."

Reduction of overall costs

A reduction in labour costs is not necessarily an essential requirement for a productivity agreement. In most cases a reduction in total operating costs is being sought, and in all cases an examination of the total cost situation should be taken into account. One of the objects of the agreement might well be a saving of materials (Chapter 10 gives an example of a scheme devised for this purpose). Another important source of savings is increased machine utilisation or reduction of capital assets employed. The following two examples show this aspect.

Example 1

A production study of one department revealed poor machine utilisation, which was mainly due to the ineffectiveness of the operators. Further investigations revealed high labour turnover in the department, which was traced to a low level of pay. The type of man being attracted was on the whole of insufficient calibre to be effectively trained, and hence did not make the grade. He was frustrated in his inability both to cope with the machine and to achieve acceptable earnings. The agreement specifically set out to increase the levels of pay, and hence the labour costs, but the overall cost of production was considerably reduced.

Example 2

This is an example with many parallels. At any given moment there are parked at the transport cafés of the country millions of pounds of capital equipment in the shape of vans and lorries being under-utilised. Usually the simple explanation is the low *rate* of pay of the drivers, who thus have to put in more time to make up an acceptable level of earnings. Increasing the rates of pay, and usually the earnings, in exchange for agreed measures or shift working can considerably reduce the number of vans or lorries required. With petrol tankers, for instance, costing up to £15 000 each, the potential savings in spite of increased labour costs is very significant.

Six

Sociological Analysis

If, twenty years ago, it had been suggested that there was a need to examine the attitudes and expectations of employees when contemplating major workshop changes, practical managers would have looked askance. But before then, in the 1930s, the Hawthorne experiments had shown the significance of the social organisation of industry, while industrial psychologists were beginning to probe the nature of man's motivation at work. Today, there is widespread recognition that a company is a complex socio-technical system and that the attitudes, expectations and loyalties of the various groups have a substantial impact on a company's performance.

It might be thought obvious that a detailed productivity agreement should take account of these attitudes and aspirations of the employees affected by any major changes contemplated. In fact they are frequently recognised only in terms of the increased earnings offered. Of course, employees' economic needs are significant and are tending to increase in a materialistic society. But they are not exclusive.

There are two aspects of these changes which may be viewed as opposites. One is negative as far as management, supervision and employees are concerned: the uncertainty and insecurity which are induced. The other is positive: the opportunity the agreement provides to correct the inequities of the existing situation and to improve relations, financial benefits and working and employment conditions.

If the agreement is to cover both aspects properly—to give reasonable reassurance on the one hand and opportunity for fulfilment on the other—it is necessary to find out what the specific situation is. For example, how secure do employees feel in the company? What are the major complaints about payment systems or employees' relations with management and supervision? How much trust is there between them? Are shop stewards leaders of, or controlled by, their members, and what do they see as their objectives? These and a range of other questions should be explored. The information obtained from an analysis of the situation will provide a guide in determining the scope of the agreement and the means by which it can be implemented. How is this information obtained?

Use of the attitude survey

Employees' attitudes should be probed on a systematic basis. The views of the managers, supervisors and shop stewards involved should be similarly covered. The most effective way of carrying out such an analysis is through a carefully designed attitude survey, preferably undertaken by an experienced and well qualified third party. Managements who have carried out such surveys themselves have frequently, and understandably, encountered bias in the answers they received from their employees, since the latter do not feel completely free to express their views. The survey is of little value unless such inhibitions are removed. Respondents must feel able to talk freely and frankly, secure in the knowledge that the results of the survey will be presented in such a way that complete anonymity is guaranteed.

Usually a representative random sample of employees is selected—generally 10 per cent or more—and in addition a large proportion of shop stewards covering all departments and shifts in the plant. Each individual in the sample is then interviewed by a member of the survey team and the interview follows a prescribed course, set out in a questionnaire, a copy of which is in front of the respondent during the interview. A typical example of one of the questionnaires is given in Appendix 3. Each questionnaire is drawn up in relation to the specific needs and situation of the individual company and these are established after discussions with management, supervisors and shop stewards. A draft is prepared and tried out in a small pilot exercise; it is discussed with managers and shop stewards, and then a final version of the questionnaire is agreed.

The questionnaire will cover, in most cases, the following aspects of employees' attitudes to the company and their expectations and views about any changes that may be made:

1   Employees' expectations about their work and its rewards.
2   Employees' overall opinions of the company.
3   Current wage systems and incentives, including levels of pay in relation to the area and employees' expectations.
4   Attitudes to management and supervision.
5   The effectiveness of communication channels in the plant, particularly between management and the shop floor.
6   Hours of work and shifts, with particular reference to overtime levels.
7   The role of the unions and shop stewards.
8   The pace and variety of work.
9   Employees' understanding of, and attitude towards, company values.
10 The degree of understanding of productivity.

The writers have carried out surveys of this type across a range of large- and medium-size companies in all parts of the British Isles. Each questionnaire was designed to take account of the specific situation in the company and reflected the requirements of the individual managements and shop stewards.

Examples of survey results

Most questionnaires have a similar structure and, as these investigations have generally been carried out in the course of feasibility studies prior to the development and negotiation of a productivity agreement, certain questions are common to many surveys. In order to demonstrate the range of results obtained from companies in various parts of the country, with differing industrial relations situations and with varied management philosophies and organisation, we have extracted the results from four such surveys over a range of questions.

All such surveys contain two types of question seeking to elicit employees' attitudes and opinions. There are open-ended questions, to which the employee gives any answer he considers appropriate in view of his attitude to the subject raised—for example, what are the good/bad points of working for XYZ Company?

Alternatively, there are forced choice questions, where the respondent is presented with a statement and asked whether or not he agrees; for example—"The management here really knows what it is doing"—*Agree/disagree/don't know.*

52

Questions of the latter type are more readily analysed, but suffer the disadvantage that they do not reflect differences of opinion unless the range of replies offered is widened. To some extent, these questions channel the respondents' opinions into specific areas which the questionnaire wishes to explore. The open-ended question, on the other hand, gives the respondent complete freedom to explain his reply, his preferences and his attitudes.

Figure 6:1 shows the results obtained in four attitude surveys to an open-ended question asking respondents to describe the good and bad features of the company for which they worked. For obvious reasons the identity of the companies has been concealed, but the region of the country in which they were situated is indicated. To point up the differences, it should be observed that each company is in the engineering industry. Companies A and B were part of a large group, and each of the factories in which the surveys were carried out employed 500–2000 workers, so that in each case comparison in terms of size is possible.

An analysis of the results shows that there were both similarities and major differences between the opinions of employees in the four companies. Among the similarities to be found listed in the good features of each company are security of employment in three cases, while fair wages and the accessibility of the factory were each mentioned in two cases. On the other hand, there were differences in the good features. In only one case was the willingness of the management to listen to employees mentioned, although considerate supervision was raised as a significantly good feature in two instances. The same samples also mentioned poor supervision—indicating the impact of the supervisors' role in those companies were an apparently variable quality. Employee facilities and benefits were mentioned only in the company in South Wales.

An examination of the bad features mentioned by the samples in each of the four companies also reveals similarities and distinct differences. In each case, working conditions were mentioned as one of the worst features. In three of the four, payment and wage levels and structure are mentioned. The exception, Company D, had levels of pay well above the national average and, indeed, above market rates in the particular area. It is interesting to note that in companies C and D, production disruption and problems and the planning of work were mentioned as significantly bad features of organisation which affected employees, but they were not mentioned in either

Company *A* or Company *B*. In the latter two companies, lack of action by management or poor communications were regarded as notably poor features—a fact which would have significant implications for the negotiation of a detailed productivity agreement. Perhaps most important of all was the fact that in only one company, *C*, were relations between management and employee regarded as a particularly bad feature. Even this, in the case of Company *C*, was apparently mitigated by the fact that supervision was seen as "considerate." In this case there is no doubt that management had a major problem in changing its approach and in obtaining a greater degree of acceptance of company objectives from its work-force. This is something a detailed productivity agreement may provide the opportunity to undertake.

Figure 6:2 is an analysis of the results from a number of forced choice questions again taken from the attitude surveys for the four companies concerned in Figure 6:1. In these replies, even more significant differences between the four companies are apparent. If one examines the profile of Company *A*, for example, as compared with Company *C*, a very different picture emerges. In Company *A*, employees were ready to admit that, under the present system of payment, some men did not really earn their money. This is frequently the case in companies which have chaotic wage structures, with piecework systems which have become slack. This was not the case in Company *C*'s situation at the time of the survey, but relations between management and employees were poor, as shown by the answers for this company in Figure 6:1. Moreover, in this company far fewer employees admitted that some men were not truly earning the money they took home. In fact, management had its wages system under reasonably close control. In Company *A* the indications of better industrial relations are plain to see, but at the same time clear evidence of an inequitable payment system is revealed in the answers to question 5.

In Company *A* there was ready acceptance of the fact that work has to be measured if the company is to be efficient. This attitude is interesting to compare with the result in Company *B*, which was situated in an area more traditionally inclined towards piecework. In the latter, employees did not see the payment system as equitable, a position which differed from attitudes in Company *A*, where the wage system was on the whole felt to be reasonably fair, despite the fact that earnings varied too much.

	Company "A" (North)	Company "B" (West Midlands)	Company "C" (South Wales)	Company "D" (Midlands)
1 Good features (in order of frequency mentioned)	(a) Management listen to you (b) Easy pace of work (c) Left alone to get on with job (d) Good management (e) Security	(a) Closeness of factory to home (b) Friendly work-mates (c) Security/ steady employment (d) Considerate supervision (e) Left alone to get on with job	(a) Fair wages (b) Job security (c) Considerate supervision (d) Employee facilities	(a) Position and accessibility of factory (b) Lack of pressure (c) Fair wages (d) Friendly work-mates and atmosphere (e) Hours of work
Total number of good features mentioned	11	231	35	144
2 Bad features (in order of frequency mentioned)	(a) Working conditions (b) Money scale/ differentials wrong (c) Lack of action by management	(a) Working conditions (b) Wages/pay levels (c) Poor communications management and supervision (d) Poor supervision (e) Men not treated as individuals	(a) Relations between management and employees (b) Production disruption and problems (c) Poor supervision (d) Working conditions (e) Pay/wages structure	(a) Efficiency/organisation/ planning of work (b) Working conditions (c) Standard of supervision
Total number of bad features mentioned	56	171	52	85

FIGURE 6:1 ANALYSIS OF EMPLOYEE ATTITUDES

Question	Company A (North)			Company B (West Midlands)			Company C (South Wales)			Company D (Midlands)		
	Agree %	Disagree %	Don't know %	Agree %	Disagree %	Don't know %	Agree %	Disagree %	Don't know %	Agree %	Disagree %	Don't know %
1 Under the present system of payment some men don't really earn their money	77	23	—	43	45	2	38	62	—	69	29	2
2 Things have to be actually measured if the company is to be efficient	95	4	1	55	43	3	—	—	—	88	9	3
3 The employees usually get a fair deal from management	71	27	2	77	20	3	60	40	—	91	7	2
4 You can get a fair wage under the present system	69	31	—	21	79	—	27	70	3	77	23	—
5 There is too much variation in earnings	25	75	—	—	—	1	11	86	3	17	80	3
6 You never really know what is going on here	54	46	—	52	38	10	40	57	3	—	—	—
7 What do you think of your current level of pay?												
Good	9			8			22			—		
Reasonable	49			46			46			—		
Below average/poor	42			46			32			—		

FIGURE 6:2 ANALYSIS OF EMPLOYEE ATTITUDES

Replies to sample questions shown as percentage of total respondents.

In the three companies where information was available, it was clear that employees were not very impressed with the quality of communications, particularly in Company *C*, where, as we have already commented, relations with management were regarded as poor. The more detailed information obtained from open-ended questions is also demonstrated in Figure 6:2 in the answers to question 7, "What do you think of your current levels of pay?" Take Company *C* as an example. Only 27 per cent of the employees felt they could get a fair wage under the current system of payment. However, in answer to question seven, 68 per cent of the sample said that their current levels were either reasonable or good—a higher proportion under these two classifications than in Companies *A* or *B*. In detailed attitude surveys such differences are probed by a variety of interlocking questions, for simple forced choice questions are unreliable. Important aspects of employees' attitudes are, therefore, examined under a number of headings so that differences of attitude and the bias produced by answers are fully explored.

The results provide a guide to the major aspects of any productivity agreement and, overall, give the lie to the common management impression that all employees are seeking is as high a level of earnings as possible for as little work as possible. Employees are primarily interested in security of employment, stability of earnings, good working conditions and interesting jobs. They are prepared to accept high performance levels and, in most areas, targets or standards to work against, provided these are fair and provided they do not become a management instrument for imposing harsh and rigid centralised control. On the other hand, employees *do* view major changes in working practices with some initial suspicion, and these surveys emphasise the importance of a comprehensive communications programme using as many channels as are available to management in order to obtain employees' understanding and acceptance of the changes proposed.

Finally, one further aspect of attitude surveys should be mentioned. We have rarely experienced opposition from employees or their representatives in undertaking these surveys. Employees apparently welcome the opportunity to talk frankly and openly with an unbiased third party about all aspects of their employment. Their participation in surveys of this kind establishes a measure of employee goodwill towards the changes which management is hoping to make. The survey is a tangible expression of management's intention

57

to consult employees and to obtain their co-operation in carrying out the changes. If for no other reason, a detailed attitude survey of the type described (and exemplified in Appendix 3) is well worth undertaking.

Consultative machinery within the company

As well as the attitude survey, there are other aspects of the company's existing industrial relations climate which should be studied and analysed. One of the most important areas in this respect is the existing communications structure (if any), which is designed to provide a channel of communication between management and the company's employees. Many companies have joint consultative machinery which has been in existence for years. In our experience, few of these consultative bodies are working effectively, yet the need for improved communications is evident whenever one studies industrial relations problems. Equally evident is the need for a communications plan, using as many channels as possible, to obtain employees' agreement to the programme of change inherent in a comprehensive productivity bargain. A critical appraisal of existing channels is therefore essential.

If the present joint consultative machinery has fallen into disrepute, the consequences are at least two-fold. First, employees are likely to be suspicious of any management proposals for change, because they will seem to be a reversal of the old policy under which managers failed to keep employees informed or to use the consultative machinery to initiate new ideas. The primary reason why industry is littered with the corpses of so many works councils is that management has not seized the opportunity which consultative machinery provides. Analyses of the minutes of such works councils generally show that managements leave the responsibility for raising matters for discussion to the employees' representatives. Employee representatives are, therefore, cast in a role which encourages them to raise grievances and to make complaints. They are not encouraged to think constructively nor to seek identification with the growth and prosperity of the company.

Second, a completely redesigned communications structure will usually be necessary as an important feature of the productivity agreement. This is covered more fully in Chapter 14, but the implication here is that management should plan how it intends to obtain employees' agreement in the light of past failures to communicate its aims and views to them. This failure may have been due to lack of initiative, attitudes that are out of date, or to poor management training. Whatever the reason, attitudes will have to be changed.

Evidence of labour turnover

A detailed analysis of the incidence and pattern of labour turnover also reveals information about the employment situation in a company and the extent of employees' satisfaction with the existing work situation. The numbers and types of employee who have expressed their opinion by "voting with their feet" provide quantitative evidence of the present situation.

For example, heavy turnover amongst employees of less than six months' service often indicates weakness in induction procedures and in training methods. Restricted opportunities for progression into higher-level jobs can give rise to heavier turnover after longer periods of service. On occasions it may be found that turnover amongst longer service employees has suddenly increased from a certain point in time. This is significant and needs investigating. Two principal reasons have been found which may be interrelated:

1   The failure of the company's level of earnings or wage–effort relationships to keep pace with those in the area. This may occur particularly in companies whose wages systems are under effective control, and where experienced employees cannot bargain for increases.

2   A deterioration in the industrial relations climate of a company with little tradition of employee militancy, or with weak union membership. In such cases, employees do not take industrial action. They leave. If such symptoms are not diagnosed and remedial action taken, militancy is likely to appear.

High labour turnover represents a substantial cost. It can be measured in terms of:

1   Recruitment and selection expenses.
2   Administrative and induction costs.
3   Wage costs of learning.
4   Costs of recovering lost production and spoilage costs.

In addition, heavy turnover has other effects which defy accurate costing, for example its effect upon employee attitudes and morale.

A recent estimate of the costs of labour turnover, by the National Economic Development Office, puts the cost per leaver for female employees in the rubber industry at £70. Other studies suggest that this is a conservative figure and that in some instances such costs can be as much as £400 per leaver. There may therefore be substantial direct savings if labour turnover can be reduced. The implementation of a productivity agreement will often provide an opportunity to tackle this problem.

Other areas of investigation

We have indicated some of the principal areas of investigation when carrying out a sociological analysis of a company. There are others— for example, the nature and frequency of employees' recourse to the established grievance procedure and the types of dispute which arise. Companies vary widely in this respect, and objective study of the negotiating situation can highlight the nature of existing company–employee relations. A detailed analysis of the minutes of two negotiating committees in one large engineering company revealed that:

1   Almost all items were raised by the unions. Out of 205 items discussed in a two-year period, only seven were raised by management.
2   There was much more regular union than management attendance. In one committee, meetings were characterised by the absence of a third of the management members.
3   Wages and conditions amounted to 26 per cent of the subjects covered, welfare facilities 30 per cent and safety 18 per cent. From the lack of items raised by management, it appeared to regard the committees as having little real value. Many of the items raised were so trivial as to be inappropriate to the seniority of those attending the committees.

It appeared that union members were doing their best to make the committees work, but were faced with a marked lack of enthusiasm on the part of management—a situation confirmed by the delays which occurred in taking action on matters raised.

There was widespread dissatisfaction with the effectiveness of the committees which confused negotiating and consultative matters and produced conflict as well as a sense of frustration between the groups attending. Such failure to distinguish between questions on which trade union advice is being sought and those which can be settled only by negotiation is common to many organisations. It invariably leads to a situation in which all items are negotiable, and a co-operative, constructive relationship proves impossible to achieve. This kind of situation needs to be radically reformed before a detailed agreement is implemented.

If the discussions between management and shop stewards about the productivity agreement are structured correctly, two of the main objectives of the exercise can be achieved: to obtain some convergence of managerial and employee objectives, and to bring into being a more constructive relationship. Analysis of the sociological situation will ensure that the agreement takes account of (a) what employees expect from the company, (b) the degree to which there is misunderstanding between them and management and (c) the means by which it can be reduced. Finally, it will shed light on the problems of change—both in attitude and in conditions of employment—which are necessary to increase productivity, reduce unit labour costs and create a more satisfying work situation.

Seven

Analysis of the Wage System and its Effects

For many companies, the problems of controlling productivity and labour costs are centred on their wage structures and payment systems. A comprehensive productivity agreement will often have as a major objective the rationalisation of the wage structure and the introduction of more appropriate, more effective bonus systems.

Need for a detailed wage analysis

Whatever the form of the company's existing wage structure and payment systems, they are likely to have contributed substantially to the creation of its industrial relations climate and to have affected the way managers and supervisors undertake their man-management responsibilities. This influence represents an important aspect of the initial study and calls for a detailed analysis of the wage structure and its effects. The analysis should cover:

1   The earnings levels of, and differentials between, employees in the job population.
2   The wages structure's contribution to, or effect upon, performance levels.
3   The extent to which the present structure affects management in utilising employees efforts to the full.
4   The degree of managerial control of the structure, and the extent to which it facilitates employee pressures on management or creates conflict.

The analysis should not be carried out too cursorily. If accurate information is not obtained, the resulting proposals are likely to prove inadequate. Errors or omissions can lead to expensive mistakes when a new, rationalised structure is put forward for negotiation. Unexpected increases in labour costs could result—but after management and unions have completed their negotiations, there is generally no going back.

The detailed requirements of the wage and earnings analysis are: that it should be comprehensive and accurate, and that the information should be collected in a manner which permits a variety of analyses to be made with speed and simplicity. One of the most difficult parts of data collection is obtaining accurate wage and earnings levels. Another is that even when the information is obtained, there is uncertainty about its interpretation and therefore about its value. The following sections cover these aspects.

Technique of wage analysis

The information should satisfy the following criteria:

1 It must cover all employees in the job population under review

Information is required about what each employee earns and how each is paid. Everyone will want to know specifically how any agreement will affect him (or her). As employees will want to be satisfied individually about proposed changes in their earnings level, incentive arrangements and level of overtime, an individual analysis is the only possible means of obtaining the necessary information.

Other needs—in this case of management—underline the need for individual analysis. Management must know accurately what costs are involved (and what savings may be anticipated) from implementing new proposals. Approximations and estimates are likely to cause problems at the negotiating table.

2 It must cover a sufficiently long period

This is to provide an accurate picture of employees' earnings and must take account of recent changes in rates of pay, and so on. To ensure that it is accurate and relevant, information should be extracted over a reference period. One or two weeks is too short for this purpose. That fortnight might have been anomalous in terms of overtime level or short time working, for example, or it might have been a "bull" week just before the annual holidays.

On the other hand, the reference period should not be excessively long. If it is over a year the information is likely to be out of date, particularly if wage increases have been negotiated or there has been wage drift. It is better to take two shorter reference periods of one month, separated by nine months or a year, than a single twelve-month one—which in any case would mean a long process of data collection.

Three months is probably the most suitable reference period in most instances. It should be as recent as possible but should avoid any unusual periods, such as holidays, short-time working or other factors which would prevent it from being representative.

3 *It must distinguish clearly between the major components of gross earnings*

For each individual the earnings analysis should cover:

(a) *Gross earnings.* To include premium earnings for overtime and shift work. The levels of pay to be negotiated in the productivity agreement in relation to any projected increase in productivity must take account of the established earning expectations of employees. A substantial increase in pay for a basic forty-hour week may still prove unacceptable if high overtime has become established and a substantial reduction in total "pick-up" is contemplated under a new agreement which proposes to abolish systematic overtime.

(b) *Total hours worked.* The aim of the productivity agreement is to increase the productivity of the work-force. This aim may be achieved by increases in production proportionate to the rise in productivity, provided that the production can be sold. Alternatively, it may be attained by a reduction in the total man-hours worked or by a combination of both factors. In reducing the gross man-hours worked, a reduction in overtime levels may provide the first means of absorbing increased productivity, particularly if the alternative is redundancy. In many cases, overtime has become an established means of providing employees with satisfactory earnings levels. In some areas of the country, employers quote a guaranteed level of overtime as a recruitment incentive. Unfortunately this affects the tempo of work in the factory and results in loss of managerial control over employees' hours of work.

(*c*) *Forty-hour earnings.* This figure is simple to obtain for staff employees but often very difficult for those who are hourly paid—a commentary on the complexity of many companies' wage systems. The main use for these figures is to provide a basis for comparison and negotiation, which must take place on a readily understood and logical basis. The forty-hour earnings figure provides this basis and may be quoted, compared and negotiated as either an hourly or a weekly figure according to company tradition and employees' views.

As already mentioned, comparison and negotiation based on the forty-hour figure may lack realism where overtime and shift premiums are an important component of gross earnings. Negotiations on forty-hour earnings figures may make it appear that the company is being generous in its offer and the size of this increase sometimes gives managements much concern. In one example, a company offered rates of pay which gave employees an average of 19 per cent increase in forty-hour earnings. The negotiations were long and difficult, and employees' reception of the proposals was unenthusiastic. They had for many years worked, on average, 15 per cent overtime, and the new forty-hour level seemed to them a poor deal, since their gross pay was reduced considerably.

The information required for a detailed analysis of the wages and earnings of employees may be summarised as follows. For each employee in the total population under review, over an appropriate reference period:

1   Job number or code.
2   Basic rate or grade rate an hour.
3   Gross average earned rate an hour/a week.
4   40 hour average earned rate an hour/a week.
5   Average overtime premium.
6   Average shift premium.
7   Average hours a week.
8   Range of earnings (to show fluctuations).

Gradually companies are computerising their payroll calculations and where this is the case, this information is (or should be) readily available. In other instances, the information should be put on to punched cards for ease of analysis.

Differentials in the existing wage structure

The detailed information obtained from the individual analysis of earnings over a suitable reference period provides a means of examining the actual structure of differentials in the company, factory or plant. Wide variations in earnings levels are the rule rather than the exception. They take little or no account of the inherent responsibilities and skills of the range of jobs in the job population. Within a group of similar jobs—for example, skilled, semi-skilled, and so on—earnings on a forty-hour basis may vary by more than 100 per cent, revealing major inequities in the existing structure.

Examples of forty-hour earnings levels for a large job population are shown in Figures 7:1 and 7:2. Both are taken from the engineering

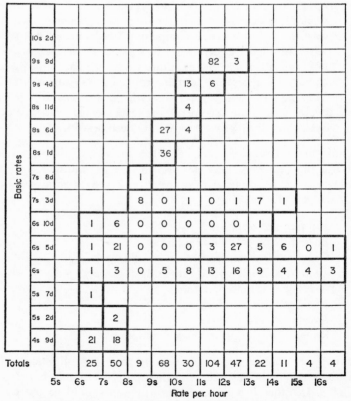

FIGURE 7:1   DISTRIBUTION OF EARNINGS: COMPANY *A*

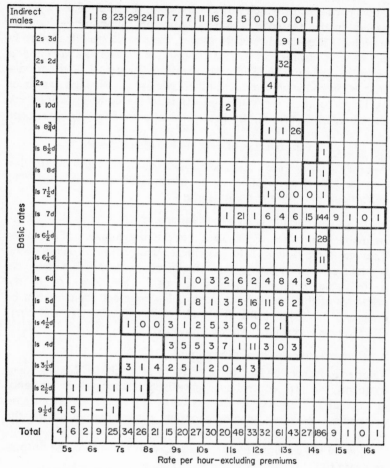

FIGURE 7:2   DISTRIBUTION OF EARNINGS: COMPANY *B*

industry and are not untypical of the actual situation in engineering concerns which have relied heavily on the national agreement to define their wage structures. The figures in these tables come from an actual company and have not been selected as a particularly extreme example.

The problems of rationalising such structures are dealt with in Chapter 11. Here the method of presentation should be commented upon. Forty-hour earnings for all individuals are plotted against an appropriate factor which broadly indicates the level of work undertaken. In the examples, this is a basic rate, superimposed on the nationally negotiated rates. In theory, these rates are intended to be reflected in earnings levels so as to provide a rational and equitable series of differentials. The cost of rationalising such a situation—that is, introducing equitable differentials—can be high: as much as 12 per cent of the wages bill. It is in the company's interests, therefore, to do this within the context of a productivity agreement.

Effectiveness of existing incentive schemes

Another aspect of the wage and earnings analysis is an investigation into the effectiveness of incentive schemes, where these exist. The constituent parts of the analysis are:

1 What schemes are currently in existence?

In many companies there are a bewildering number of schemes. They are the product of the piecemeal introduction of payment-by-results systems over many years, of revisions by production managers or industrial engineers, of concessions to employees or to the pressures of the local labour market. No coherent principle can be discerned to account for the multiplicity of schemes, and their effectiveness is certain to vary enormously.

2 How effective are current schemes?

Their effectiveness or lack of it, needs to be analysed. Management frequently has little control over incentive schemes; pay performance and actual performance levels may be widely separated. Reports on companies' incentive schemes contain paragraphs of which the following is typical:

"Since 1960 earnings have increased, with no increase in output, as a result of:

(a) Granting additional allowances.
(b) Extra operations booked largely on the basis of the operators' own estimates.
(c) Loose standards through insufficient study, or method changes not recorded.
(d) Bargaining on new standards in order to obtain an earnings opportunity consistent with the current level. (This is serious because standards as a result bear little relation to work content.)"

Shop-floor bargaining is, of course, a perennial problem with payment-by-result schemes, and although many companies try hard to separate the establishment of standards and the level of pay associated with the standard, one frequently finds situations like the following:

> "Although from January 1964 a clear distinction has been made between the functions of the work study department, to set standards, and the personnel department, to set the wage rates, it has proved to be largely illusory in practice."

Thus the effect of existing schemes must be analysed carefully as far as earnings levels and wage drift are concerned, and related to the results of the production analysis described in Chapter 4.

The pattern of earnings can reveal significant information about productivity restraints or the extent to which the work-force controls output levels. Where, under supposed piecework or incentive working, the bonus pay of substantial numbers of men is within $2s$ ($10p$) a week of each other, there is—putting it mildly—a strong indication of restriction of output. On the other hand, wide fluctuations in the same departments usually indicate that the standards are arbitrary.

Analysis will reveal the extent of any shortcomings in the current wage structure and the various payment systems. Where major weaknesses are identified, companies should examine the whole basis of their remuneration policy for manual workers. In the following chapter we therefore describe a number of payment systems which are currently in operation, and subsequently some basic principles of financial remuneration. Decisions on the way in which it is proposed to reward employees in the future will have a major effect upon the scope of any productivity agreement which is subsequently developed.

Part III

DESIGN AND DEVELOPMENT
OF A WAGE SYSTEM

8	*Current Systems*	73
9	*Model Principles*	86
10	*Design of Components*	96
11	*Rationalising a Wage Structure*	115

Eight

Current Systems

A detailed examination of the wages and earnings situation will probably reveal one or more of the following three major defects:

1   The operation and control of the system are ineffective. For example, the earnings levels do not reflect real differentials, whether these are formally established or not.

2   The system does not contribute sufficiently to the total motivational pattern. In many cases it actually acts as a disincentive.

3   As a system it is incomplete, for example, there is no mechanism within it for increasing earnings levels.

These defects manifest themselves in many ways; they arise from an inadequate conceptual framework for remuneration policies and practices.

Together with an effective communications structure, the development of comprehensive remuneration policies and their translation into practice constitute the main foundations of the productivity agreement. In this chapter some current systems of wage payment will be described. The two following chapters will explore the principles on which more effective systems can be founded and describe the translation of these principles into the design and restructuring of wage systems.

Effectiveness of payment-by-results systems

Before describing the more common systems, or family of systems, of wage payment in use at the present time, we should note the controversy surrounding the effectiveness of financial incentives and payment-by-results (PBR) systems. Influential and vocal strata of industry and some academic circles condemn direct financial incentives for shop-floor workers. They argue that payment-by-results systems:

1   Lead to wage drift which managements cannot contain.
2   Have an adverse effect upon the quality of line management and supervision, who tend to become progress chasers and to abrogate their managerial functions.
3   Lead to narrowness of outlook and attitude on the employees' part, promoting resistance to change and restrictive practices.
4   Are inconsistent with the aims of an industrial organisation, which should integrate all its members' activities to make the organisation as effective as possible.

On the other hand, many managers, employees and indeed consultants are wedded to the use of direct incentives. They can often point to dramatic increases in productivity and a continued high level of employee activity as proof of the effectiveness of payment by results. Report number 65 of the Prices and Incomes Board, *Payment-by-results Systems*, mirrors this divergence of opinion. One senses that it is with some reluctance that the report comes to the conclusion that: "We are on the whole satisfied that conventional PBR systems can be a useful tool for raising effort in situations of low performance." [Chapter 10, paragraph 245.] In the final analysis the report hedges its bets—"we cannot, therefore, make a general commendation or condemnation of conventional PBR systems"—and provides an important list of criteria by which the success of PBR systems should be judged (see Appendix 4).

It is a pity that the sheer number of reports produced by the Prices and Incomes Board has meant that this one received less attention from management than it deserved, despite the fact that the Board's chairman, the Rt Hon Aubrey Jones, emphasised its importance when it was published. It provides the first analysis in any depth of the effects of financial incentive systems on British industry, and underlines the need to examine carefully the type of work involved and a range of other criteria before a company decides the type of wages system it should introduce. It urges companies to analyse the effects of their current systems of payment and commends alternative systems for consideration.

Such analysis is urgently needed in many companies, particularly those which have introduced incentive systems within the framework of national agreements (for example, the engineering industry) and failed to establish accurate, objective measurement standards as the basis of the incentive payment. This latter problem arises in a wide range of industries. Performance standards are frequently the subject of negotiation on the basis of "mutuality"—that is, mutual agreement between the individual and the company representative about the performance standard. As a result, it is the hardest bargainer who earns the most, rather than the hardest worker. In such cases managements are subject to continual pressures and lack any factual basis on which to ensure equitable differentials in relation to job worth and individual or group performance.

PBR in action

Coventry "mutuality"

This situation exists at its most clear-cut in the Midlands, particularly in Coventry. Mutuality appears to be an article of faith for Coventry car workers and their unions, as at least one of the major manufacturers has discovered. A comparison of earnings levels between Coventry and Birmingham, only 16 miles (26 km) distant, will show how this insistence on mutuality has benefited the Coventry worker. Which is not to say that the employer always suffers as a result, for there is widespread agreement that the employees work hard and, having made their "price," generally fulfil their part of the bargain.

From one aspect, therefore, Coventry exemplifies one of the themes of this book: that until recently too much attention has been paid to earnings levels and too little to labour costs. Other things being equal, companies can and should pay high wages *if* they can generate high levels of productivity from their employees. Companies should become more competitive between themselves in this respect, and if the Government's incomes policy does nothing else, its erosion of the reliance of employees and unions alike on the principle of "comparability" will have had a beneficial effect. For this reason, one of the Prices and Incomes Board's criteria for productivity agreements—that "companies should avoid setting payment levels which are extravagant and which might provoke resentment outside"—is both disappointing and largely irrelevant.

While Coventry's high earnings and productivity are what employers and employees should all be seeking, the basis on which they are achieved is not an example for others to copy. The Coventry system facilitates conflict between management and employees and allows sectional interests, in the form of small groups of key workers, to exert excessive pressures on a company. It inhibits change in working methods and leads to unofficial strikes or management weakness, as companies lack objective standards on which to base pay and performance levels. Thus negotiations resemble the haggling of an oriental market, and power is wielded in confrontation situations by groups of employees who have discovered the advantage they hold.

A detailed analysis of this situation presents so much that is potentially disruptive that it is a tribute to the moderation of both sides that abuses are not more widespread and wage drift not more acute. A traditional balance and ingrained sense of values seem generally to prevent an explosion. Unless there are radical changes in the accepted means of determining pay and productivity relativities, however, more serious conflict is likely as Coventry feels the effect of increasing international competition.

The efforts being made to tackle the problems of pay, performance and wage drift in Coventry by the Rootes Group Limited since Chrysler gained control suggest that, as a result of such outside influences, solutions may be found which are rational and fair. They will centre on the introduction of an appropriate system of payment, and on union agreement to objective standards of measurement.

There is a requirement for recognition on both sides that "mutuality" represents a form of joint regulation of the wage effort relationship which is now out-dated and leads to chaos. An alternative form of joint regulation at an organisational level higher than that of the individual will be of real "mutual" benefit.

Coventry's difficulties highlight the problems associated with payment-by-results systems and explain why they have been so widely criticised. Other problems identified by the Prices and Incomes Board can be summarised as follows:

1   Technological advances and improvements in methods and organisation produce increases in earnings under PBR systems quite independent of the increased effectiveness of the work-force. (Note that this should not be taken as a denial of employees' right to share in the benefits of increased

76

efficiency. But any such share should be defined on a logical basis.)

2   Insufficient attention is paid to the "learning curve effect." This increases earnings with long production runs as standards become progressively looser and employees do not accept, or management does not attempt to introduce, revised standards. Again, it should be noted that the effect of the learning curve is to improve employees' efficiency, and they ought to share in the benefits. The difficulty is maintaining control and determining their share accurately.

3   The practice of guaranteeing the earnings of the previous task when negotiating a new task raises earnings and labour costs, but not output, per employee.

4   The bargaining process associated with the fixing of new piece rates or work standards pushes up earnings according to the power of shop stewards or the degree of pressure employees exert rather than according to output levels.

5   Earnings gains are inequitably distributed. The anomalies disturb differentials within and between sections, departments and divisions, creating further bargaining pressures.

In an attempt to overcome at least some of these problems, other wage systems have been introduced.

Measured and controlled day-work

These systems of payment are a means of establishing a contractual relationship between management and employees, to relate payment to performance levels and secure mutual adherence to a set of rules governing performance. For an agreed rate per hour the employee agrees to maintain a stipulated level of performance. If this level is not achieved, the employee retains his agreed rate of earnings until it has been clearly established that the failure is his own responsibility and is not due (for example) to faulty materials. Only then is the employee warned, his rate of pay dropped, or other suitable action taken. The principal difference between *controlled* and *measured* day-work is that, under the former system, only one performance level— and hence one level of pay for any given job—is established, whereas the latter involves a range of performance levels and rates of pay.

Professor Tom Lupton of the Manchester Business School has

argued that under this system the employees still exercise a degree of control, but in a different way. They are fully involved with management in deciding what the rate for the job should be and what is a "reasonable stint." This latter point is perhaps debatable if the work can be accurately measured, using, for example, synthetic time standards such as MTM. Employees would have to be convinced of the fairness of the standards of performance, however they were derived.

A change to this system of payment from conventional payment-by-results cannot be accomplished successfully without careful preparation. Other motives than the purely financial one are relied upon to act as incentives under a measured day-work system. The employee is asked to recognise a certain obligation based on the equity of the reward for his work.

Such a system has numerous repercussions on the managerial structure of the company. A carefully designed procedure must be implemented which will provide accurate and up-to-date information on the performance of each section and department. Management and supervision will be responsible for ensuring that contracted performance standards are maintained and that employees are not kept waiting for materials, tools or whatever. An increase in the supervisory establishment will probably be called for, as the supervisor's role is enlarged beyond the progress chasing which is his major function under most conventional PBR systems.

In order that accurate control information shall be quickly available to line management, each department requires a cluster of specialists to provide the data, process it and, where necessary, assist in taking action to solve any problems that are thrown up. These specialists might comprise an industrial engineer, a production controller and, in some instances, maintenance engineers. They are necessary because, with a specific level of pay for defined amounts of work, control of labour costs is firmly in management's hands. Quick diagnosis of sub-standard performance and prompt action are necessary if labour costs are not to escalate.

A well-known example of this type of payment system is the "Premium payment plan" operated by the Philips Electrical group of companies. Its basic principles are as follows:

1   All jobs are classified according to their difficulty and complexity by means of detailed job evaluation.

2   Where work is measurable, a predetermined motion–time system is used to set operation times, from which operator performances are calculated on a 60–80 scale (where 80 is standard performance for the motivated employee).

3   Within each classification, job rates are established for the range of performance from 70–90 in steps of five points. These job rates are paid for all hours of attendance, as shown below:

PAY STEPS	PERFORMANCE STEPS	JOB CLASSIFICATION
1	Training	[A, B, C, D, E, F, G, etc
2	Training	(as determined by job
3	Training	evaluation)]
4	70	[Amount paid]
5	75	
6	80	
7	85	
8	90	

FIGURE 8:1 PHILIPS PREMIUM PAYMENT PLAN

Each major plant has its own training school where new operators are trained. During training, an operator is paid the rate for the appropriate job classification at the lower end of the performance scale. Training continues until a 70 performance has been reached and maintained for two weeks at a satisfactory quality level. Thereafter an operator may elect to raise his performance above 70 and so increase his earnings. Once an operator has accepted a performance target, the company expects it to be honoured, and detailed checks by the work study department are carried out on a regular basis.

If an operator fails to meet his contracted performance, his pay level is not reduced until management has established that the reasons are entirely within his control. Even then, downgrading is not immediate and the employee is given a reasonable time to try and regain his performance level.

The problems associated with this type of system were revealed in a detailed analysis which the company made after it had been in operation for a number of years. The analysis covered 12 000 workers and examined the responsibility for failures to meet contract performance level. The results may be summarised as follows:

FAILURE TO MEET CONTRACTED PERFORMANCE LEVEL

Operator responsible (condoned):	2 per cent
Operator responsible (actionable):	8 per cent
Management responsible:	25 per cent

This study shows the extent of the pressure on management to reduce its responsibility for employees' failure to meet their contracted performance level. The greater their failure, the higher the company's labour costs will be, and a weak, inefficient management could rapidly put itself out of business by introducing such a system.

Measured or controlled day-work calls for an appropriate management structure and sophisticated, speedy control information. It should be applied only to companies whose products are mass-produced or made in large batches. Finally, it needs a consistent and appropriate method of work measurement, expertly applied.

Graded hourly rates

This system is really a carefully designed form of merit payment. It is used principally to provide an incentive in the payment system when objective measurement standards cannot be established. It is also used more widely by certain companies, often subsidiaries of American concerns, which have established universal employment conditions for all categories of employees.

An example of this system of payment was introduced, with the assistance of Associated Industrial Consultants Limited, in parts of a major engineering group. Three- or four-hourly rates of pay were established for each main occupational group—fitters, electricians, welders, and machine operators. In each category the employees are graded by their supervisors according to a number of factors, each of which has a total number of points available. The most important aspects of the employees' performance considered are: skill, rate of work (assessed against measured standards), and quality of work. Additional factors such as diligence, time keeping and reliability are also assessed, permitting the payment of an additional amount on top of the graded hourly rate. (See Appendix 5 for an example of the assessment form.)

This system gives the foreman the basic responsibility for rewarding his men according to the skills they bring to the work and the degree of effectiveness with which they are applied. It thus enhances the foreman's responsibility and helps to focus his attention on his man–management responsibilities. The foreman discusses the individual's performance with him at six-monthly or yearly intervals and tells him his grade for the following period. As a result the foreman is directly responsible for the development of his subordinates, so the system has the advantages (and drawbacks) of the merit rating interview.

Graded hourly rates are most appropriate for highly skilled groups of workers who undertake a wide range and variety of work. Even so, they suffer from the subjectivity of the assessment and from the difficulty such systems labour under—however carefully devised and punctiliously administered—of appearing fair and just to the people they are applied to. Accusations of "favouritism" may be overcome to a large extent by introducing appeals committees, with equal management and shop steward representation and a non-voting chairman. Employees who feel they have been unfairly assessed can appeal to their committee. The members do reach agreed decisions and are valuable as a communications channel through which management and shop stewards can discuss and explore each other's values. The safeguard of an appeals committee with a membership structured in this way is, we believe, essential.

By and large, however, the application of merit rating schemes is limited to the higher ranges of hourly paid employees, where skill and task complexity are at a premium. Even at this level they must be designed with care and implemented with tact if they are not to have an unsettling effect upon those paid by the system, and so lead to lower morale and lower productivity.

Plant-wide incentive schemes

British companies have shown relatively little interest in plant-wide incentive schemes, except those with a conventional output basis. The schemes are often appropriate to certain single-product, single-operation industries where the production processes demands flexibility from the workers. In the United States there has been more widespread acceptance of schemes covering a company or factory, most of them using or deriving from the concepts of the Scanlon plan or the Rucker plan. The fundamental idea is that employees are paid a collective bonus, based on an overall assessment of labour productivity measured in financial terms.

Conceptually, these schemes resemble profit-sharing schemes. Both the Scanlon and the Rucker plans reflect a recognition by management of the need to give employees a tangible stake in the enterprise. Hence they merit consideration in the light of the increasing pressure, visible in all advanced industrial nations, for a greater degree of worker participation in companies' affairs.

Plant-wide schemes, superficially at least, appear to provide a better framework for integrating the efforts of the work-force with the company's objectives than the traditional profit-sharing approach. They reflect the contribution of the work-force to company prosperity more directly and more clearly. Profit sharing is subject to fluctuations outside the control of the company and its employees. The experience of a major British car manufacturer is not uncommon: in 1967 it paid out no profit sharing bonus, although it had produced the largest number of vehicles in its history without a proportionate increase in its labour force or other resources. When this occurs, the traditional profit sharing scheme falls into disrepute with employees.

Plant-wide incentives are based on a ratio of labour costs to sales, added value or some similar index of company performance. Under the Scanlon scheme, the ratio varies and is of secondary importance to the sociological climate which must be established to gain employees' involvement and co-operation. While this is a crucial factor in any plant-wide scheme, the Rucker model and its derivatives place greater emphasis on the measure of employees' productivity, finding it in the ratio of labour costs to added value.

In many companies the ratio of labour costs to added value is relatively constant. The Rucker approach is based on the assumption that there is, in fact, a constant relationship between labour costs and output—that there is a fixed proportion of company revenue which is the normal entitlement of the labour force.

This assumption is an over-simplification and may be a prime cause of the failure of plant-wide schemes to gain much acceptance in Britain. Labour costs are not wholly variable in relation to the added value produced by a company, and differ from material costs in this respect. They are more properly regarded as "semi-variable," containing both fixed and variable elements. Analysis of this ratio for major British companies over the past few years has revealed:

1   The relative stability of the ratio of labour costs to added value in the majority of cases.

2   Large increases or decreases in the added value produced by a company are accompanied by similar but less marked changes in the company's labour costs.

This latter phenomenon is not surprising. It will not be news to production managers that employees work more effectively and apply themselves to greater effect when the order books are large and schedules are high. On the other hand, the tempo of work decreases when orders fall off and schedules are reduced. In the latter situation, managements react comparatively slowly to a fall-off in demand by curtailing recruitment, reducing overtime or negotiating redundancies. If the labour force is skilled, or labour scarce, such steps may lead to the company losing many of its best employees. Managements naturally proceed cautiously, and in any event are subject to pressures from their employees' unions when contemplating such steps.

Thus the semi-variable nature of a company's labour costs must be taken into account in devising the basis of a plant-wide scheme. It is perfectly possible to devise mathematical models which identify the relationship between added value and labour costs, and which provide a measure of labour productivity in terms of improvements over established trends in this basic relationship. This more sophisticated measure establishes a more accurate basis for plant-wide schemes and is currently being introduced by several companies.

While financial measures are commonly used as the indices for plant-wide incentive schemes, physical output measures may in some cases provide a simpler and more accurate index which is readily understood by all employees. The simpler the index the better, as far as the motivation of employees is concerned, and physical measures satisfy this requirement best.

Where there is little variation in product mix, or where labour flexibility can take account of the differing work content of a range of products, then a single measure can be used, such as tons produced in a foundry or total footage drawn through a tube mill. If a range of factors and/or products affects the determination of productivity levels, more sophisticated indices are required. They can frequently be developed with the help of statistical techniques—notably multiple regression analysis, which establishes the interrelationship of a group of factors as determinants of productivity performance.

Implications of plant-wide schemes

Plant-wide incentive schemes may be viewed as the opposite end of the spectrum to individual payment-by-result incentives, both motivationally and as reflections of company philosophy. They reflect the need of the enterprise to integrate the activities of the work-force in the cause of co-operative endeavour. They specifically recognise that the organisation must achieve results from its employees greater than the sum of their individual efforts. Individual payment-by-result incentives, on the other hand, tend to set the employee up as an individual entrepreneur, selling his effort to the company in accordance with mutually agreed terms—terms which, in many cases, are constantly being renegotiated. However, their impact on the individual can be powerful and may provide a strong stimulus to increased productivity.

The most frequent criticism of plant-wide incentives is that they fail to take account of the individual's overriding desire to benefit solely from his own efforts. Unless a system of payment provides for this motivating individual need, its incentive value—it is alleged—will be minimal. According to this school of thought, employees will apply themselves diligently only if they alone benefit from their efforts, and are not asked to share the results of their labours with others.

This view is an over-simplification. It stems in part from managers' tendency to transfer their own opinions, which derive from environmental experience, to the work-force. Managers inhabit a competitive world, to which they have been conditioned from their youth—in many cases from birth. By and large, they have inherited, or their early environment has encouraged, competitive instincts. They passed examinations at school, gained places at university and have obtained promotion at work in competition with others. They are not only used to competition and the rewards associated with individual achievement: they believe it is a natural law which governs attitudes to work and life itself.

But the shop-floor employee has been through a different kind of environment. He did not pass those vital examinations to grammar school and university. His opportunities of promotion are limited and those that do exist are often obtained through length of service. His strength is not his individual ability, but his power in combination with his fellow workers. His experience therefore fosters adherence to group norms of behaviour and reliance on co-operation with his fellows to achieve desired objectives. This is not to deny that he is also motivated by personal drives which he seeks to satisfy through his own individual efforts; merely to recognise that they are less dominant than management's.

Thus the motivating factors which plant-wide incentive schemes seek to release among employees are as significant as the individual drives traditional incentives rely upon. Each system, in fact, satisfies some of the total motivational needs which financial incentives can, in part, satisfy. In later chapters we shall be examining the feasibility of devising payment systems which reflect both the individual and the group needs of employees, thus providing a more comprehensive and effective framework of financial motivation, which in turn substantially assists the optimisation of employees' overall performance.

In conclusion, the advantages of plant-wide incentive schemes may be briefly summarised. They are:

1   The economic discipline, as regards wage costs and productivity, which the system inculcates in employees.
2   The improved communications and increased sense of participation which a successful scheme engenders.
3   The separation of pay performance from work study, which facilitates the continued improvement of methods, layouts, etc.
4   Their relative simplicity and low cost of administration.
5   Properly devised schemes are non-inflationary, since increased earnings are a result of the improved utilisation of company resources.

These are proper objectives for any system of payment, and should be sought by managements at all times. Many systems in use today meet none of these requirements and hinder the effective motivation and utilisation of the labour force. Basic principles of remuneration are discussed in the following chapter.

Nine

Model Principles

It is convenient to consider initially the principles of remuneration in terms of expectations. There are on the one hand the expectations which the employee desires to be satisfied. These can be described as conforming to external criteria such as a standard of living and earnings levels consistent with his market value and to internal criteria relating to differentials, to contribution made, skill requirements, and so on.

The company, on the other hand, expects to be able to recruit and retain the calibre of personnel required to carry out its operations and to obtain high standards of performance, flexible working arrangements, and the like.

Expectations in common

Some of these expectations conflict and some do not. Common to both is the expectation that the system should be in accord with the importance of the roles within the organisation. Industrial organisations are hierarchical in structure and are composed of designated tasks or groups of tasks which are described as jobs or roles. Each role is expected to make a defined contribution towards company objectives and is created to satisfy a need which the company has identified in order that it may meet its commitments and pursue its aims satisfactorily.

These groups of tasks or jobs are, however, theoretical and meaningless unless, and until, they are undertaken by an individual. The individual brings appropriate skills, knowledge, experience, and personality to the job which a company requires to be undertaken.

The jobs vary in scope, complexity, and so on, and each of them prescribes or limits the individual occupying the position. Its scope and the degree to which its occupant is prescribed or limited in carrying out its responsibilities are two of the major determinants in selecting the individual to undertake it.

One of the reasons, it is claimed, why these jobs, or groups of tasks, are organised into a hierarchical structure is the distribution of talents and abilities in the human population. Thus industrial and other organisational structures have a pyramidal shape whereby the largest number of jobs and job occupants lie at the base of the organisation structure. Those at this base are responsible for carrying out the basic function of the enterprise, be it the production of goods, the rendering of services, or, in a military organisation, fighting battles. Those in more senior positions are, in one sense, servicing these basic members of the organisation, but in another sense are their leaders, obtaining through leadership a greater contribution from the integration of individual efforts than would be the case if each individual was working solely on his own.

Whatever the reason for this type of organisation structure, it is a fact that jobs or groups of tasks vary in complexity in relation to their position in the structure and that a starting point for the remuneration of any group of people working in an organisation should be the nature of the job. Put another way, this means that the foundation of any remuneration policy is the establishment of a job–worth element which will seek to establish an agreed set of differentials between the jobs at various levels and in differing functions across the organisation.

Importance of differentials

It is sometimes said that all problems connected with payment in industry are basically problems of differentials. While this may be an over-simplification, there is no doubt that such problems are a major cause of pressures upon payment systems and of disputes between employees and management. Probably the most incisive and integrated analysis of this problem of differentials has been carried out by Dr Elliott Jaques in his books *Equitable Payment* and *Measurement of Responsibility* (Heinemann). Jacques says that "there exist shared social norms of what constitutes a fair or equitable payment for any given level of work, these norms being intuitively known by each individual." He claims that the totality of these social norms

87

about equitable payment levels provides the basis for establishing an equitable series of differentials in relation to differences in the level of work carried out by individuals in the jobs which they occupy within industrial organisations. This concept of the individual's feelings about the level of pay which is fair, and its consistency across the population in relation to the level and type of work carried out, is most useful.

Equally important is the relationship which Jaques identifies between level of work, individual capacity, and level of pay as the basis for the feelings of individuals about equity or lack of equity in their payment system. When these three elements—the individual's capacity or ability, his level of work, and the amount of pay he is receiving—are in balance the individual, Jaques claims, is satisfied in terms of his motivation, both financial and non-financial. Whenever any of these three elements becomes seriously out of balance, frustrations occur, and the individual's performance may suffer or management may find themselves subjected to pressures either on an individual or group basis. Jaques also claims that the individual's capacity increases in his working situation over the years and notes that while staff and management structures sometimes provide for pay increases to maintain pay and capacity in some sort of balance, few wages structures do. In many instances, there is little provision for increases in the level of pay for employees on the shop-floor to match their increase in capacity. For example, a tradesman completes his apprenticeship at twenty years of age and is, therefore, theoretically regarded by management, and indeed by his union, as being able to perform a range of work similar in scope and technical complexity to that undertaken by a craftsman of twenty years' experience. In fact, of course, the inexperienced craftsman does not undertake the most difficult work in the maintenance section or tool room, this being left to the most highly-skilled and -experienced members of the team. The systems of wages payment in industry for such categories rarely reflect this shop-floor reality. This suggests that there is a need to provide a variable element which, as the individual's capacity and contribution increases, also increases his pay.

Variable element in remuneration

The problems encountered with financial incentive systems have been indicated previously. Most of these problems, however, arise from

88

either the inadequacies of the particular system or from incorrect application and insufficient control. It is the effects of these which have been attacked and which have led to an attack upon the principles. Our position can be stated quite simply as follows:

1   The principle that in an economic environment there should be some financial reward related to achievement, is sound and sensible.
2   Financial incentives have an important contribution to make within the total motivation pattern.
3   There is now sufficient experience, knowledge, and understanding to enable effective systems to be designed and applied.

What then are the characteristics required of a variable element? In the first place it should be related as closely as possible to the contribution required of the job holder. This requires an accurate job specification with properly defined objectives related to unit objectives. Unless this is done the proper measure or measures cannot be determined. It also requires a careful analysis of the system within which the work is carried out so as to determine the size of the group to which the measures should be applied. This group should be as small as possible, consistent with the operational pattern.

It should be noted, however, that individual incentives are becoming less and less appropriate to most operations. Apart from their undesirable induced behaviour patterns, individual incentive working usually requires, for example, too many work-stations with probably buffer stocks. It is very rare to find situations where the work is completely controlled by the individual. Where there is a high degree of this control it is recommended that an individual element is introduced combined with a group element.

A second requirement of the variable element is that the reward for achievement should be significant but not excessive. Too little will not elicit the necessary response; too much will lead to excessive pressures on the system. The design of the system, including the variable element is discussed later, but as a rough guide it is suggested that the earnings should have a potential variability of about 20 per cent. This variability, however, should not be applied over a short term.

An important requirement of an employee is predictability of earnings. Thus the changes in payment depending upon the performance should be effected at not less than four-weekly and prefer-ably twelve-weekly intervals. Although the performance is calculated weekly the average over four weeks determines the level of pay for the next four weeks, and so on. For similar reasons slight variations in performance should not affect pay. Performances can be banded or stepped in units of say 5 per cent.

A third characteristic is that the variable element should be directly related to the established differentials and should enable these to be maintained. One of the real problems of piecework systems is the gradual erosion of standards for many reasons, improving methods, learning effect, etc. A device which has been used in the past is the imposition of a limit on earnings.

The effect of this has been usually to eventually limit production. In some factories the work-force, having produced their "stint," stopped work two hours early.

A more effective way of controlling the situation is to have a limit for any single incentive unit and to syphon off the results of perform-ances above this into a pool which is used to raise the whole wage structure at periodic intervals.

Of course one of the real problems of a variable element is its application to situations which cannot be measured. Measurement problems based upon the use of statistical techniques and financial ratios where direct measurement is inappropriate have already been commented on. These techniques are capable of widespread applica-tion. Where, however, even these are inappropriate, properly ad-ministered personal assessment schemes should be introduced. It is important however not to use spurious measures and it is usually desirable, where measured and non-measured systems are in opera-tion in one unit, to have a differential in target earnings of say 5 per cent between the two.

Finally, it must be emphasised that variable element schemes, of whatever kind, are only part of the total industrial relations system. They are an integral and interacting part of the total motivational pattern.

Share-of-prosperity element

So far we have established the need for two elements in a wages system; a basic component related to job worth which is part of an equitable system of differentials, and a variable element which will stimulate the employee's performance in the important features of the role. These two elements combined should establish a level of pay which matches his reasonable expectations. However, a further component is necessary—"a third tier." There are of course a number of companies at the present time who have a third component which takes the form of profit-sharing, annual bonus or even perhaps occasional "conscience-money" payouts. These are usually arbitrary, very remote, and have little motivational effect. At least one large company recently, which, having a profit-sharing scheme but no profit, paid out a bonus in lieu of profit-sharing bonus!

What then are the arguments for a third-tier? They fall into two broad categories which can be classified as sociological and economic.

The sociological argument is that all employees are entitled to a share in the prosperity of the unit in which they work. Over and above the skills and abilities they bring to the job and the performance they achieve they are expected to contribute more. The individual exists within the organisation and is expected to some degree to subordinate his self-interest to the interest of the company at large. The company requires loyalty and a degree of identification from its employees. It requires co-operation, good housekeeping, flexibility of working, and the like. The employee also needs to identify himself with the unit quite apart from perhaps running his own little business within it. There are obviously counter arguments to this. The subject is an interesting one for debate and a third-tier cannot be justified on these grounds alone, although they have some merit. A far more convincing argument can be put on other grounds.

The first argument is for the third-tier as a means of control. Most wages systems are only partially within the control of the unit. Basic rates are negotiated at national level, earnings levels are mainly determined by "going rates" in the district. Increases in most industries are still negotiated and imposed on a national basis, irrespective of the circumstances of an individual company.

Managements can therefore exercise control only by ensuring that the numbers of people employed are a minimum consistent with effective operation. This raises the important distinction to be made between earnings levels and wages costs. This distinction has not always been made and managements and governments have tended to think in terms of keeping earnings down. There is of course a simple relationship between the two—that is, the earnings levels multiplied by the numbers employed give the labour costs—excluding labour attracted costs. The control is on labour costs, or, more correctly, on total operating costs of which labour costs are a more or less significant part. In other words management has not much control over how much to pay out certainly as a minimum, only over what is obtained for it. This minimising of costs is achieved by motivating employees to a high performance or effective machine utilisation, maximum material yield, and so on. Ideally labour costs should be related to the performance of the unit and increases in earnings achieved through increases in this performance. There are, however, problems of measurement and of application.

In Chapter 8 Scanlon-type schemes were outlined. These offer some of the characteristics we are seeking. However, they are in themselves, limited in application and require particular economic conditions.

The principle of using "added value" can be adopted and used very effectively as a third tier.

Added value component

Let us now describe the added value component in more detail. In considering relationship of time factor with "added value," a number of variables can affect the ratio by having an influence on the added value, such as:

1   *Selling price.* Any changes in selling price will—if the other variables remain constant—affect the added value. However, it is usual to find that price adjustments are a result of some change in the variability of labour or materials and therefore are compensated for in the added value calculation.

2   *Raw material costs.* Fluctuations in raw material costs are generally reflected in selling price changes.

3   *Capital expenditure.* It is often believed that the introduction of plant and equipment that will increase production and cause a reduced unit labour cost will affect the relationship between direct labour and added value. This is often the case, but if there is a means by which the employees benefit from the resultant increased productivity, they will show a greater willingness to have the new equipment introduced and operated efficiently. Where such a factor does have a significant effect upon the index it can be allowed for by adjusting the index after the equipment is in full production.

By using the relationship between direct labour costs and added value as a productivity index, changes in productivity can be measured from the fluctuation in the index in many ways, but predominantly in the following:

1   Increasing saleable output with the same resources—that is, increasing the output in the time available.

2   Better utilisation of materials by the saving of scrap and rejects and by the employees' acceptance of more effective quality control standards.

3   Greater co-operation in the introduction and manning of new equipment—particularly equipment of a labour-saving nature.

However, by using direct labour costs as a percentage of added value, any savings in indirect labour will not affect the index, although it would affect the profitability of production. A tendency could arise to classify employees as indirects rather than directs, and thus improve the index. To overcome this situation, it would be preferable to use a ratio of total labour cost to added value and then any savings in indirect labour would improve the ratio. Where staff are included, the ratio would be total salaries and wages to added value.

So far this is the way in which added value is used in Scanlon type schemes and its disadvantages have been described. Most of these disadvantages can be eliminated or considerably reduced by using the index, not as a determinant of a bonus share-out but as an annual improvement factor. Thus the index is determined and a target index based on it agreed. If this target is achieved then the whole wages structure is raised by say 5 per cent. Variants can be introduced of, for example, increases of from 4 to 7 per cent if there are tolerances on the target. The target should be set for a period of not less than two years, preferably more, say between three and five years.

Effectiveness of added value index

This method of using an added value index as a determinant for wage increases has many and quite widespread implications.

Firstly, it introduces an element of economic realism into the wages system since it allows for a controlled increase in earnings. It should be noted that where a national award is made this is paid as agreed. The ratio is not altered, however, and thus the increase is paid for out of the increased prosperity. This assumes of course that the index is improved beyond the effects of the national increase, but this improvement can be either by increased efficiency or raising prices. Under the simplest method of application described above the increases in earnings have already been paid for by the previous year's performance. Usually some interim payments are introduced during the year—for example, a holiday or Christmas bonus at, say, half-rate which is then consolidated at the year end. When the increase or consolidation occurs again the ratio is not altered and hence, to achieve the target for the following year, increased performance has to be achieved.

Secondly, although it is not a financial incentive in the normal sense, it encourages measures to improve methods, save materials, and to effect improvements in all operational areas. The implication is, of course, that the work-force, or other participants are entitled to a share of all improvements whether they are responsible or not—for example, increases in prices. Provision can be made for some items to be excluded, for example, it may be considered desirable to extract a given return on capital employed from the calculations. This does not always have the effect intended, however, and several calculations should be done with different suppositions introduced. Schemes have been introduced with the third tier based, for example, on contribution for each clock hour, but in general terms the further the index is removed from realism the less satisfactory it becomes.

Thirdly, the third tier is an important part of the communication structure. It will not be effective by itself; it acts as a focus of attention for real discussions on overall productivity and is a central theme for the productivity panels discussed elsewhere. The work-force and other participants are invited to share in and make contributions towards overall prosperity. This obviously implies that all kinds of decisions, some of which may be considered purely the prerogative of management, will be questioned. It is left to managements to decide whether they are prepared to justify or defend their actions in the open. If they are so prepared and if they also use imagination in translating their actions into terms meaningful to the work-force, they will be astonished at the response. They will find that many of the problems which they have had for a long time disappear, not because they are resolved, but because they become irrelevant.

Fourthly, and perhaps most important from the point of view of wages systems, the third tier gives a high degree of stability. Given that the amount of money to be paid out is what can be afforded in real economic terms, the distribution of it becomes a matter of fair administration and joint regulation, since increases in one section are gained at the expense of everyone else. Apart from the negotiations, every two or three years, of the target index, the problems connected with wages are substantially reduced and are mainly concerned with the maintenance of the established differentials. There is also a common objective in ensuring that work standards are kept fair so that the same effort throughout the unit is required for the agreed share.

This chapter has presented what we believe to be a very substantial case for a three tier wages system based upon agreed job worth, performance-based variability, and a share in prosperity element which is also a real economic parameter. This system has many arguments for and against. Those against, however, are mainly theoretical. The practical arguments—that the system works, is better than most other systems, and is not difficult to apply—are overwhelming. The practical design of the system is discussed in Chapter 10.

Ten

Design of Components

It is not claimed that the three-tier system is the perfect wage system, with universal validity. The principles and characteristics can be applied over a wide field of industrial and commercial activity, but they must be adapted to suit particular circumstances. The wage system must be designed to work in the situation the feasibility study has uncovered, both in the shorter and in the longer term aspects. It may not be possible, or desirable under some circumstances, to introduce all three elements. It is usually desirable to introduce at least two, even though they may be combined—as, for example, the combination of job worth and variable element—into a measured day-work system. When designing a new wage structure, however, it is convenient to consider the three elements—job worth, variable performance and share in prosperity—separately.

Evaluation of job worth

The foundation of a properly designed remuneration structure must be the establishment of acceptable differentials between different levels of jobs (or tasks) within the same job population. To meet this criterion, many companies are introducing graded payment structures, which set out to group together all jobs of similar worth or responsibility. These graded structures are successful if:

1   The grading of jobs conforms to the general opinion of job worth within the company (*internal* differentials).
2   The corresponding job rates of pay for the grades are reasonably well aligned with market rates (*external* differentials).

3   Any performance component in the structure is accepted by the job occupants and is seen to be fairly administered.

If these criteria are satisfied, the more common disputes about payment are unlikely to arise.

The process of grading the jobs is the foundation of a successful remuneration structure. It is carried out by one of the various job evaluation techniques. A number of methods have been developed for comparing the worth of different jobs. [For a description of various job evaluation methods, see job evaluation report number 83 of the National Board for Prices and Incomes, September 1968.] While no one method has become universally used, probably the most common is that based upon a "factor plan." Under this method, a number of points are allocated to a range of factors selected to cover the most important requirements of the job population which is being evaluated.

The factors vary according to the job population. Managerial jobs are assessed against such factors as "supervisory responsibilities," "relationships," "technical complexity," and "responsibility for decisions." For jobs in the factory, factors such as "level of skill," "responsibility for materials and/or equipment," and "working conditions" are used.

As the factors vary according to the particular job population and according to the views of those responsible for the evaluation exercise, so do the total number of points (the weighting) given to each factor. The allocation of points under the factor plan system encourages one of the major fallacies about job evaluation: that it is a scientific, or at the very least an objective, technique which introduces definitive criteria into the emotive and subjective matter of determining levels of remuneration.

Perhaps unfortunately, job evaluation does not become an objective technique merely through the attribution of numerical values to certain selected factors. The measurement is spurious, as any examination of the way factors and their weightings are determined will reveal. The usual process generally follows these lines:

1   Factors are selected by a group of managers, advised by the personnel manager. He will have chosen a suitable sample from various factor plans of which he has obtained details.

2   Points are allocated to the factors according to the subjective

views of the management group ("What we need most from our work-force is high quality work, so obviously 'responsibility for the product' must have the most marks.")

3 After prolonged discussion, the points and the definitions of the various levels are agreed for each factor and a sample of "bench mark" jobs are assessed by the factor plan. When the results are examined, they may well be unacceptable to the assessment panel. The marks for the factors are juggled about, and the bench mark jobs are re-assessed until better results ("better" in that they appear more reasonable) are obtained.

4 The factor plan is finalised and the full range of jobs in the population is assessed. Difficulties in ensuring uniform standards of assessment will be encountered, and the assessment panel may revise certain results. Eventually a rank order of jobs is established after a great deal of managerial effort and much time. Then the results are given to the job holders, and all too frequently. . . .

5 The job holders reject the results and a long process of consultation and negotiation begins.

This description only slightly caricatures the factor plan method of job evaluation. It cannot be gainsaid that some companies have taken great pains with such job evaluation programmes and have achieved satisfactory results. This has generally been due to two factors:

1 Great care in developing the factor plan and in co-ordinating the assessments.

2 More important, obtaining the participation and involvement of the job holders and their representatives in carrying out the exercise. This is achieved by getting job holders to complete job descriptions and by including their representatives on the assessment panel.

This participation is crucial in establishing any new wage structure. ["... we ourselves consider that unions should play a part in the establishment of a scheme, for this increases the chance of acceptance." PIB Report number 83 "Job Evaluation," Chapter 9, paragraph 142.]

But however much care is taken, the fact remains that the factor plan system of job evaluation is not only time-consuming but gives a spurious air of objectivity to an intensely subjective matter.

New approach to job evaluation

We believe that the whole question of job evaluation should be looked at afresh. Answers to a few simple questions may provide the means of doing so. The questions are:

1   What are the aims of job evaluation?
2   What determines the effectiveness of job evaluation?
3   What can job evaluation *not* do?
4   Who should be involved in any job evaluation exercise?

The real aim of job evaluation is easily stated. It is to place the jobs of any given job population into a rank order of importance. It really cannot do more than this. It does *not* establish a graded payment structure.

The principal determinant as to the correctness of the rank order, and therefore the effectiveness of the job evaluation system, is its acceptability—primarily to the job holders but also to their managers and supervisors. If an evaluation system produces a rank order which those affected or concerned with the jobs feel is about right, then it has passed the acid test. This has been recognised by the National Board for Prices and Incomes, which in its report number 83 on job evaluation states categorically that "acceptability is indispensable to a job evaluation scheme."

No practical job evaluation system can in itself give a financial value to a job or group of jobs—that is, it cannot "evaluate" in the strict sense of the term. Company norms vary enormously. Compare the pay of welders in various industries, for example, in relation to other skilled and semi-skilled trades. Market rates also vary enormously across the country: compare the earnings of an electrician in a steel works in the North-East with those of the same trade in Coventry or Slough. This is where theoretically interesting job evaluation systems such as Elliott Jaques's Time-span of Discretion fall down. They simply do not produce acceptable results.

The theme of employees' involvement and participation in matters which really affect them and to which they can contribute (which is not, we believe, at board level) will recur throughout this book. Employees' involvement in determining the rank order of jobs in a given job population is one such area. Experience in the design and development of new wage systems shows that if employees are not involved in determining the basic wages structure, the problems of

99

successful implementation are greatly magnified. More important in the long run is that management will have missed an opportunity to change from a policy of confrontation to one which seeks to gain employees' co-operation and to build on areas of common interest. There is no need for the question of job importance to become a subject of negotiation. The extent of agreement between management and employees is considerable, provided the means of seeking out this agreement are structured correctly.

To summarise these views about job evaluation, therefore, we suggest that:

1   The purpose of a system of job evaluation is to establish a rank order of jobs in a given job population.
2   The criteria by which such a job evaluation system should be judged is the extent to which its results are accepted by those affected by, or concerned with, the results.
3   A successful job evaluation exercise, as part of the rationalisation of a wages structure, must directly involve employee representatives.

Direct consensus method of job evaluation

We have developed a system of job evaluation which satisfies these requirements. It further possesses the advantage of speed of execution. Using the *direct consensus method*, as it is called, a job evaluation exercise can be completed in weeks rather than months. In fact, we estimate that it is up to six times shorter than those conventional methods which involve developing a factor plan. The main features of this method are:

1   The use of paired comparisons of jobs to establish a rank order.
2   The use of a computer to analyse results.
3   The full involvement of employee representatives in the evaluation exercise.

In addition, this method allows for a unique factor plan to be developed, where required, according to company values and needs. Factor weights are determined according to specific criteria, removing the usual imprecision from this exercise. The development of such factor plans is generally necessary only for very large job populations or for companies where rapid technological change means continual changes to job content. The main features of the direct consensus method of job evaluation are:

Select a representative sample from the job population. The sample should be representative of the whole range of jobs in the population. The number of jobs chosen for the sample (N) must be a prime number, and between 30–50 is probably most convenient.

Prepare job descriptions for the sample. Simple job descriptions should be prepared for the jobs in the sample, initially by the job holder. The description should clearly identify the primary responsibilities and skill requirements of the job.

Prepare comparison forms. Every job in the sample is compared with every other job in the sample so that all possible combination of pairs of jobs are included. Forms are prepared with N pairs of jobs (where N = the total number of jobs in the sample—that is, if there were 43 jobs in the sample the number of comparisons on each form would be 43. The forms are laid out as follows:

JOB NUMBER	JOB TITLE	PREFERRED JOB	JOB NUMBER	JOB TITLE
1	Instrument mechanic		2	Maintenance fitter
2	Maintenance fitter		3	Capstan setter operator
3	Capstan setter operator		4	Storeman, grade 1

The total number of such comparisons is large and is calculated by the formula:

$$\frac{N \times (N - 1)}{2}$$

For 43 jobs, therefore, there will be 903 different decisions to be made.

Select the judges. Any number of judges can take part, and in most cases between ten and fifteen is administratively convenient. The judges should comprise a balance of the interested groups—management, supervision, shop stewards and employees. It is essential that

101

judges are familiar or acquaint themselves fully with the jobs to be ranked. Visits to the job and discussions with job holders are essential to help individual judges resolve difficult comparisons.

Distribution of ranking forms. The ranking forms are distributed between the judges so that each judge is asked to assess a proportion of the total number of comparisons. The distribution of the forms is such that the consistency of each judge's assessment can be determined.

Assessment procedure. The judges are asked to prefer one job of each pair on the basis of an explicit overall criterion such as job worth or job importance. The definition must be wide and simply defined, as judges base their decision on a complex range of factors, impressions and opinions when preferring one job to another. This aspect of the system is sometimes criticised. It appears to some that the criteria on which decisions are based are too vague and inexplicit. In the majority of cases, however, judges find no difficulty in deciding between two jobs, provided they are asked to view them "wholistically" and are not pinned down by explicit and, to them, inhibiting definitions. In some cases, judges cannot distinguish between the pair of jobs and accordingly indicate a tie. Ties should not amount to more than 30 per cent of any judge's decisions. If the proportion is greater, it is evidence of lack of knowledge on the judge's part or unwillingness to commit himself. Both can and should be dealt with, either by making sure the judge obtains further information about jobs in the sample, or—if ignorance is not the reason—probing the reasons for his reluctance to reach a decision.

Analysis of the results. The scoring system which generates the rank order is similar to that used in a football league table; two points are awarded to the preferred jobs in each comparison and one point is awarded to tied jobs. This straightforward scoring system has been adapted to take account of the calibre of jobs to which any particular job is preferred. This is done by crediting each job with the total score to which it is preferred and reorganising the rank order on the basis of the new scores. This refinement minimises the effect of any eccentric decisions and reduces the random bias which may result from the particular distribution of blocks between judges. It also gives the rank order representing the greatest degree of agreement between the judges.

The rank order and degree of agreement between the judges is determined by a computer. The computer constructs a grid with the job numbers, in overall rank order, listed horizontally along the top and vertically down the left side. An example of this grid or matrix is shown in Figure 10:1.

The judges' original results (2 for a preferred job, 1 for a tie and zero for one which is not preferred) are recorded alongside the *vertical* list of jobs. This means that a decision which is in accord with the overall rank order will produce a 2 to the right of the diagonal running from the top left to the bottom right of the grid, as is shown below.

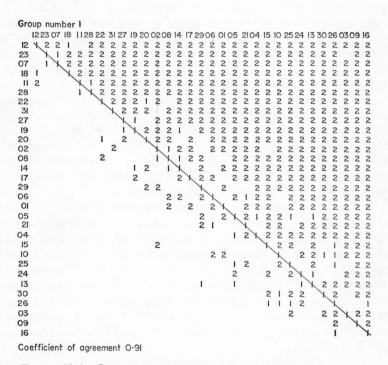

Coefficient of agreement 0·91

FIGURE 10:1   OUTPUT GRID SHOWING JOB EVALUATION RESULTS FOR THIRTY-ONE JOB SAMPLES

A decision which contradicts the overall rank order will produce a 2 (for a win) to the left of this diagonal. This decision can easily be identified, by examination of the grid, as can the judge who made the decision by reference to his completed forms.

The proportion of 2s to the right of the diagonal is consequently a measure of the agreement between the judges. The computer calculates this proportion, ignoring ties, and prints it as a coefficient of agreement—which, in our experience, is invariably above 80 per cent (0.80) and usually in the region of 90 per cent (0.90).

Effectiveness of direct consensus method

It will already be apparent that this method of job evaluation produces results quickly, but its advantages are more fundamental than that. The method is based quite explicitly on the subjective nature of job evaluation and quantifies only according to personal opinion. The careful interrelating of the pairs of jobs ensures, however, that each judge's subjective opinion is consistent—or, if it is not, that it is readily identified. The results produced on the grid quickly reveal whether a judge is showing inconsistency of judgement. When it occurs, it is invariably due to ignorance or bias.

The direct consensus method produces a rank order of jobs according to the opinion of a large panel of judges representing the interested groups. Employees' representatives are *completely* involved in the actual determination of the rank order, and not merely through the completion of a job description or through talking to assessors. This participation is of fundamental importance, and removes the results from the negotiating table.

It does so not merely because employees participate, but because the method always produces a high degree of agreement between judges representing management and employees. It is frequently a shock (generally a pleasant one) for such panels to discover that they are in almost complete agreement about the rank order of a large sample of key jobs. It brings out into the open something which consultants (who are, as such, third parties) can more easily see—namely, the large measure of agreement that exists between managers and employees about many of the fundamental issues that affect both sides.

Design of the variable element

The many books on work study published since the 1920s contain ample descriptions of the various types of incentive scheme that can be used. We do not propose to re-cover this ground here. It is, however, worth noting that most of these schemes can be represented by the family of curves shown in Figure 11:3 on page 125. The link between them is the amount of the share being offered to the work-force; for example, the traditional straight-line direct incentive curve gives all the saving in labour cost to the operators. The choice of the share depends to some extent upon the current productivity and earnings levels, or at least increases in earning expectations, but in the main upon the degree of influence which the management or the men can exert on the productivity increases in the longer term. We have found, for example, that a fifty–fifty share of labour savings, from whatever source and over a long time, can stimulate productivity in both the shorter and the longer term. In certain circumstances it can act as a substitute for the third tier.

The most important factors in the design of the variable element can be summarised as follows. We have already emphasised, and reiterate here, the importance of an accurate definition of the job in terms of the unit objectives. Second, it is important to identify the main characteristics of the system in which the job forms a part.

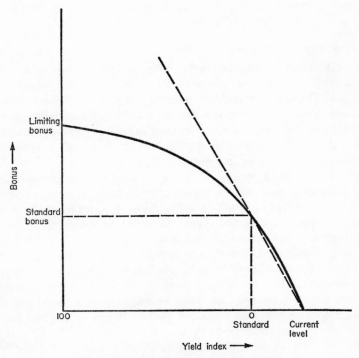

FIGURE 10:2   EXAMPLE OF YIELD INDEX

Where there is, for example, a degree of individual control over an operation but the operation is within a departmental flow system, there should be two components to the variable element. These could comprise an individual performance measurement, providing (say) two-thirds of the variable element, and a departmental index of output to man-hours providing one third.

Similarly, where material yield is important, a factor related to material usage should be incorporated. Figure 10:2 is an example of a method used to incorporate yield into a variable element. Taking total material usage as 100, a yield index for various groups of operations can be calculated. The current level of usage as measured by this index is plotted and an achievable standard agreed. The share of the savings is also agreed, and this determines the curve. In this case the agreed share was fifty–fifty, and this also gave an acceptable ratio of bonus between output and yield of 2 to 1.

Once the purpose of the task is clearly understood and the operating system accurately defined, it is usually very simple to devise an appropriate payment curve.

Accuracy of measurement

As well as the appropriateness of the measures, their degree of accuracy is also of great design importance. This is not to say that where no fine measurements are possible, the variable element cannot be used. What it *does* imply is that the accuracy of standards should be taken in conjunction with the time period of their application. Thus the less accurate the standards, the longer should be the period of performance assessment. The converse of this is also applicable: where a reasonable period of assessment is possible, the less accurate the standards need be, whether they are capable of finer measurement or not. The writers have seen, for example, work studied incentive schemes which, in order to cover all possible contingencies and variations, had tens of thousands of values. They became so complicated and so susceptible to claims for allowances for this, that or the other that calculation became not only an onerous chore but generally a waste of time, since the operator usually decided what performance he required and made out his work record to suit. One comment about a bonus system in a cable plant was "We produce performances here—not cable."

In one case we were able to reduce 25 000 values to three *and* a gain in productivity resulted. This simplification is usually possible with a return to the expression of the output in physical terms—kilos, metres, and so on—corrected statistically where necessary for product mix.

For systems which rely not upon measurement but upon assessment, the time span of application should be three to four months. Operatives should be notified by personal interview and the various factors contributing to the assessment, together with the steps required for improvement, should be discussed.

Proportionate payments

The determination of the various proportions of pay between fixed and variable elements is a pragmatic one influenced by current circumstances. As in most situations, the practical is the enemy of the perfect. The proportions also vary with the number of terms in the variable element itself. Some guidance is given in the following chapter on the interpretation of the current circumstances and their effects on wage system design and costs. Here we shall lay down general guide-lines only, and emphasise their generality.

The target earnings themselves must correspond with an acceptable wage–effort bargain. The relationship between this and the basic payments should be between 1:3 and 1:4. Smaller proportions tend to be ineffective as a financial incentive; greater proportions tend to cause excessive pressures on the standards and values.

Where there are several components and there should not be more than three, no single component should be less than about 8 per cent of target earnings.

There is usually no objection to the different elements being calculated on a different time scale, for example a departmental element calculated quarterly and an individual performance calculated weekly, with payment adjusted monthly.

The departmental performance can also be used for the payment of indirect workers. By "indirect" we imply workers whose tasks cannot be measured, as opposed to the cost definition of indirect workers as those who do not contribute directly to the operations. It is desirable to establish a differential of 5–10 per cent of total earnings between the workers who are measured directly and those who are not.

Stabilisation

The desirability that a man should be able to predict his earnings has been mentioned, and this requirement is achieved by payment over a longer time period. Stability of individual earnings can be achieved by incorporating performance bands of about 5 per cent. Figure 10:3 shows an example of this. It will be noted that the bands overlap. This is to ensure that small differences in performance—say 1 per cent—do not affect pay. A man previously on the 97–102 per cent level will not drop to the next level unless his performance falls below 96 per cent.

Stabilisation of the structure itself is achieved by limiting the earnings of any one bonus group to, say, 115 per cent and siphoning

Grades	Grade	Grade rate	1	2	3	4	5	6	7	8	Payband
Males	G	11s 9d	12s 6d	13s 3d	14s		14s 9d	15s 6d	16s 3d	17s	17s 9d	
Males	F	11s 8d	12s 4d	13s		13s 8d	14s 4d	15s		15s 8d	16s 4d	17s
Males	E	9s 10d	10s 5d	11s		11s 7d	12s 2d	12s 9d	13s 4d	13s 11d	14s 6d	
Males	D	8s 9d	9s 3d	9s 9d	10s 3d	10s 9d	11s 3d	11s 9d	12s 3d	12s 9d	
Males	C	6s 6d	6s 9d	7s		7s 3d	7s 6d	7s 9d	8s		8s 3d	8s 6d
Females	B	6s 3d	6s 6d	6s 9d	7s		7s 3d	7s 6d	7s 9d	8s	8s 3d	
Females	A	5s 9d	6s		6s 3d	6s 6d	6s 9d	7s		7s 3d	7s 6d	7s 9d
		Below 68	68–75	73–82	80–89	87–96	94–103	101–110	108–117	Over 117		Performance

Standard

FIGURE 10:3 RELATIONSHIP BETWEEN PAY BANDS AND PERFORMANCE

108

off the resulting savings into a bonus pool, which is then used for raising the whole structure. This kind of device makes the vetting or revision of standards a much less hazardous operation. It is interesting to note that in the agreement, concluded by Parkinson Cowan Appliances Limited, this vetting of standards is subject, when disputes occur, to the final decision of an outside arbitrator.

The problems usually associated with the variable element are infinitely less complicated under a third tier. The emphasis is on a fair distribution of work rather than on the imposition of management control.

Design of the share-of-prosperity element

This element requires primarily the establishment of a reasonably consistent ratio between a measure of activity, on the one hand, and a measure of performance on the other. The measurement of activity should be as closely related to the participants as possible; that of the performance as broadly based as possible.

These conditions are best fulfilled by a relationship between total wages (or wages and salaries) and added value. Other measures can be used—for example, contribution per clock hour—or the added value ratio can be adjusted—for example, to take return on capital into account separately—but the simple ratio used as an annual improvement factor is the most satisfactory. The ratio has been found to be remarkably consistent for many units and over a lengthy time period. When there have been violent fluctuations the main reasons can be traced—provided, of course, that the records are available and trustworthy.

The calculation of added value is best left to the unit accountant—not because it is difficult, since it is basically revenue minus materials. The main reason is that, depending upon the unit accounting system, the material costs bought out parts, etc, may require some calculation. Similarly, the revenue may require minor adjustments for returns—perhaps special sales discounts and the like. In any case, accountants tend to believe only their own figures! If past records are inadequate, or there have been recent radical changes (it is still worth examining the effects of these on the ratio), simple accounting procedures can be introduced which will collect the data for, say, a two-year period.

Once the added value over a period has been established, the consistency of the ratio between this and (say) total wages is examined. Any major variations should be traced. If they are the result of such things as accounting practices or perhaps sporadic deliveries, a moving average on a three-, six- or twelve-month base should be calculated. This will ensure that the ratio, which is used as a control theme for productivity discussions, is meaningful. It should be noted here that managements are sometimes reluctant to disclose financial information of this kind, and obviously some types of operation do require more confidentiality than others. When this is a problem we have invariably found that, provided the calculation of the ratio is subject to audit by the company's auditors, an index derived directly from it is acceptable to the work-force.

The next step is agreeing on the actual ratio to be used for the annual improvement factor. This can either be the simple average over the past few years, or it can be the average adjusted to take into account the movement expected from the changes in productivity and pay arrangements. The following calculations illustrate this.

The examples draw on the following background data. From past results it has been determined that the total labour cost (that is, direct and indirect hourly-paid employees) should never rise above 22 per cent of the value added to materials during a twelve-monthly period. This value has been determined from a reference period in which turnover was £7 000 000 producing £2 280 000 of added value. The total labour cost is £501 600, which represent 22 per cent of the added value. In these models it is proposed to distribute to the employees 50 per cent of the labour savings over a twelve-monthly period, and the distributions are to be made as a permanent increase in employees' basic rates. The company retains the other 50 per cent savings, and should also derive savings from more efficient operating.

Model 1

Assuming a 20 per cent increase in production and a 10 per cent increase in labour cost (it is assumed that the additional production can be sold).

Turnover increased by 20 per cent to:	£8 400 000
Giving an increased added value of:	£2 736 000
Total labour cost increased by 10 per cent to:	£551 760
Annual improvement factor is 22 per cent of the added value produced (22 per cent × £2 736 000):	£601 920

110

Therefore there has been a saving in total labour
cost, in comparison with the annual improvement
factor, of: £50 160
The employees' annual increase to basic rate would
be 50 per cent of the savings—that is: £25 080

£25 080 represents an overall labour cost increase of 4.55 per cent.
If, during the following twelve months, the added value produced
remained the same and the labour costs were constant at £551 760
plus the £25,080, then the annual improvement in basic rates for
that year would be £12 540, or an overall increase in labour cost of
2.18 per cent.

In this model it has been assumed that no adjustment was made to
the annual improvement factor for the expected increase in productivity from the new proposals.

Model 2

If amendments are to be made to the ratio of total labour cost to
added value, to encompass the new proposals, then the results of
Model 1 would appear as follows:

By increasing turnover by 20 per cent and total
labour cost by 10 per cent, the added value
would be: £2 736 000
And the total labour cost: £551 760

The resultant ratio of labour cost to added value would be 20.2 per
cent. For every one per cent improvement in the ratio, there would
be a saving in total labour cost of approximately £5500 which, if
distributed to the employees on a 50–50 basis would give an increase
in basic rates of £2740, or an overall wage increase of approximately
0.5 per cent. As a percentage of basic rates this would be greater.

Model 3

Assuming that sales cannot be increased but the increase in productivity is 20 per cent and the increase in adjusted labour cost is
10 per cent.

Turnover remains constant at:		£7 000 000
And the added value remains constant at:		£2 280 000
By increasing productivity by 20 per cent,		
the labour cost would be:	401 280	
Plus 10 per cent increase in labour cost:	40 128	
Giving a total labour cost of:		£441 408
Annual improvement factor is 22 per cent		
of the added value, or:		£501 600
A saving in labour cost of:		£60 192
Employees increase to basic rates would be		
50 per cent of the saving in labour cost, or:		£30 096

Which represents an overall increase in labour costs of 6.82 per cent. If, during the next twelve months, the added value remained the same and the labour costs were constant at £441 408 plus £30 096, then the annual improvement in basic rates for that year would be £15 048, or an overall increase in labour cost of approximately 3.2 per cent.

Model 4

If amendments are to be made to the ratio of total labour cost to added value, to encompass the new proposals, then the results of Model 3 would appear as follows:

Added value of turnover of £7 000 000:	£2 280 000
Labour cost anticipated:	£441 408

Thus the ratio of total labour cost to added value would be 19.35 per cent. For every one per cent improvement in the ratio, there would be a saving in labour cost of approximately £4400 which, if distributed to the employees on a 50–50 basis, would give an increase in basic rates of £2200—an overall wage increase of approximately 0.5 per cent. As a percentage of basic rates, it would be greater.

These models illustrate the effects on the added value ratio under different conditions. The choice of the actual ratio and its use as an index will, of course, depend on the particular circumstances of the unit, but the following rules for guides may be helpful.

The National Board for Prices and Incomes is reported to be expecting an annual increase of $3\frac{1}{2}$ per cent in average earnings. For the purposes of designing an annual improvement factor, this figure can be taken as a minimum, since:

1   Past experience indicates consistent failure to tie earnings to national "norms."
2   Trade unions will demand this as a minimum.
3   As an average, it contains categories of workers who will receive no increase at all, or a much smaller one than this.
4   There is an advantage in having a positive objective—that is, beating the national average—rather than a negative one—that is, not exceeding the average.

We suggest, therefore, that the scheme should be designed to provide an increase of 6 per cent per annum in earnings (with alternative levels of $3\frac{1}{2}$ per cent and 7 per cent for worse or better achievements respectively). Assuming that the numbers employed remained constant, this would imply a 6 per cent increase in the wage bill. Thus it is necessary to aim for the creation of a fund or "pool" of this size.

An example of the significance of a direct ratio follows. Total production value for three years—that is, total value of sales less value of direct materials purchased—was £4.5 million; gross wages paid totalled £1.9 million. The actual ratio of wages to production value was therefore 42 per cent. Had dependent labour charges been included, this ratio would have been 44.3 per cent.

To increase individual earnings by 6 per cent without exceeding the ratio a maximum must be set for total wages which can be expressed as:

$$\frac{\text{Actual ratio}}{106} \times 100$$

This becomes the target ratio; if the actual ratio is at or below this figure, the specified increase of 6 per cent becomes payable. The target ratio corresponding to the net ratio of 42 per cent above would be 39.6 per cent.

On this basis, the whole of any improvement between 42.0 and 39.6 per cent accrues to the company; the company also benefits by any improvement below 39.6 per cent, less an amount equal to 42–39.6 per cent. A more flexible arrangement can be provided by the insertion of an intermediate target ratio and a "safer" target ratio which would give increases of $3\frac{1}{2}$ and 7 per cent respectively. These ratios would be 40.6 and 39.3 per cent respectively.

It is probable that national wage awards would become payable during the life of the scheme. If the amount paid out under the terms of such an award is included in total wages, without any adjustment of the target ratios, this will have the effect of making the higher award payable (either the nationally agreed award or the domestic improvement factor).

Finally, it must be remembered that although the annual improvement factor should be established over a two to three year period, hence involving a high degree of commitment with some risk, the control over costs which is obtained and the very real invitation to co-operate in productivity improvements amply justify the risk.

Eleven

Rationalising a Wage Structure

Preceding chapters have described the principles on which a wage remuneration structure should be based. We have suggested that manufacturing industry should establish wage structures incorporating the three tiers which have been described. Rationalising a wage structure requires two things:

1   A specific framework for the redesign of the structure.
2   An understanding of the problems which will be encountered and the means of resolving them in implementing the change.

We have outlined the framework; in this chapter we shall examine, with illustrations, what is involved in making the change and how the difficulties that will be encountered may be overcome.

First, however, we would emphasise the problem of presenting a detailed programme. In the interests of clarity and comprehension, the work involved has to be set out step by step, so that it can be clearly followed and understood. This will give an impression of order and rigidity which is quite at odds with experience. This programme of implementation must be seen in the context of an intensive period of negotiation, consultation and communication with employees. Accordingly, it will be subject to the delays and difficulties which these generally entail. The problems of negotiation will be examined in Chapter 15. The programme of implementation set out below must be seen not as a straightforward exercise, but as an integral part of a comprehensive agreement designed to restructure the industrial relations of the company and the attitudes and motivation of those concerned.

115

The requirements for a successful change in an organisation's wage structure are:

1   A detailed earnings analysis over a suitable reference period, as described in Chapter 7.
2   A job evaluation exercise which establishes an agreed rank order for a large sample (or all jobs) in the job population.
3   A detailed assessment of the potential increases in productivity available (see Chapter 4).
4   Identification of the types of incentive system which are to be introduced in the new structure and of the appropriate standards by which productivity and performance levels will be measured (see Chapter 4).
5   Where appropriate, identification of the way in which a "share of prosperity" element will be used in the new structure, and of the ratio or other measure by which this prosperity will be assessed (see Chapter 10).

It will be apparent by now that detailed analysis is essential if the required information is to be obtained, and if effective performance and productivity measures are to be prepared. Assuming that the requirements listed above have been met, what is involved in implementing the change?

Defining a grade structure

The starting point for the design or rationalisation of a wage structure is the establishment of a defined grade structure. The job population should be divided into groups, or grades, of similar jobs. The earnings levels for these grades should equitably reflect the different responsibilities and demands made of the job occupants in each grade. The grade structure establishes appropriate differentials between the main groups of jobs in the job population, and provides a "career progression" for employees as their capacities develop during their employment with a company. The type of grade structure most commonly cited for manual workers comprises three basic grades: skilled, semi-skilled and unskilled jobs. Relatively few companies, however, have maintained such a simple arrangement. On the contrary, most of them lack any defined and simple foundation to their wages structure. We have come across instances where a factory of 1000–3000 employees has two or three hundred different basic rates which differ by fractions of a penny. Such complicated wage structures are irrelevant to earnings levels and realistic differentials.

The grade structure should be kept as simple as possible. For most companies, five to nine grades is appropriate for adult employees. Each grade should have a basic rate of pay which should be reflected by the grade earnings figure at target performance—that is, the additional "variable" or incentive element of pay should retain the basic rate differentials between grades. The actual number of grades into which any job population is divided must depend on the circumstances. We have suggested a range of grades for any homogeneous job population—be it manual workers, office staff or management—at this stage because, in our view, clear-cut levels of responsibility or job content should be determined pragmatically. There is no precise measurement which can distinguish accurately between groups of jobs.

Besides the coarseness of the means of measuring real differences between jobs, other considerations encourage a relatively simple grade structure:

1   It facilitates job flexibility. The greater the number of grades in a structure, the more difficult it may be to move employees to other types of work, without arguments about payment.

2   It makes managerial control of the wages structure easier, as the distinctions between the grades are clear-cut. Managements are likely to experience pressures from employees for up-grading with any grade structure. "Escalation" is difficult to prevent if there are a large number of grades and the differences between them are blurred as a result.

The actual number of grades for any given job population will depend on many factors. Among the more important will be the production processes of the unit and the range of direct and indirect jobs which these occasion; the beliefs, values and traditions of the company's management and work-force; the nature and extent of technological change, and so on. These factors differ in every organisation, and cannot usefully be considered further in a book of this nature. Each will, however, have an effect on the ultimate decision. But one of the most important determinants of a new grade structure will be the earnings levels of job holders at the time of the change. The relationship between current earnings levels and the rank order of jobs generally provides the final evidence on which a decision is made.

Analysing the basis of new grade structure proposals

The rank order of jobs produced by job evaluation is the basis of any new grade structure. We shall base our description of an approach to this aspect on a job evaluation exercise, using the direct consensus method, which has produced an agreed rank order of a significant sample of key bench-mark jobs. The procedure differs only slightly if a factor plan has been developed by means of which all jobs in the population have been assessed.

Proposals for the new grade structure should be drawn up by the team of judges (managers, supervisors and shop stewards) who have carried out the job ranking exercise. A good method is to arrange a meeting of the judges to examine the rank order, correct any anomalies and produce a final agreed rank order. The team is asked to determine a grade structure by careful examination of the rank order. In their discussions, the members of the team take into account the considerations mentioned earlier in this chapter, *except*—and this is most important—the level of earnings of the job holders. At no stage in this exercise does the joint management–employee team of judges discuss wage rates or earnings levels. These are a matter for future negotiation.

Such teams are generally able to agree on provisional grade structure proposals after two or three meetings. Frequently, "break points" are apparent in the rank order of jobs. In some cases, the total marks produced by the scoring system of the direct consensus method provide helpful information. When the grade structure has been provisionally agreed, the team of judges allocates the jobs that were not in the ranking sample to the appropriate grades. In ninety per cent of the cases there is no difficulty about this.

If the judges are unable to agree on a particular job's grade, a further ranking exercise by the direct consensus method is required. The sample of jobs would include those which have been definitely allocated to a grade and those which fall in a "grey" area between two grades. The order produced by this further ranking exercise will provide clear guide-lines as to the grade to which jobs in dispute should be allocated.

Before this exercise is completed, work should begin on examining the cost implications of the grade proposals. This will identify what the costs of rationalising the wages structure will be.

Cost of rationalising wage structure

Rationalising a wage structure will cost money. The price is generally between 3 and 12 per cent of the annual wage bill. The more anomalous the existing structure, the greater the cost of rationalising it.

The range of costs involved is initially identified by plotting provisional grade structure proposals on a scattergram, or by a similar comparative method. An example of the former is shown in Figure 11:1. In this particular company a job population of 23 jobs was placed in rank order by a team of judges using the direct consensus method. The rank order is shown horizontally across the top of the diagram, the highest ranked job being at the extreme right. The earnings of each job holder, analysed over an appropriate reference period, are represented by a dot under his actual job. The earnings figure includes, of course, incentive payments, merit bonuses and other basic elements in the make-up of each employee's pay packet.

If the distribution of these earnings is examined in relation to the rank order, the problems of rationalising a wages structure are highlighted. For example, there is a difference of nearly 1s (5p) an hour between the average earnings of the briquette preparer group and those of the mill operators, although they are placed consecutively in the rank order. The average hourly earnings of the mill group are below those of the machinists, who have been ranked ten places lower. The average hourly earnings of these machinists are well above all but one of the holders of the seven jobs ranked above them. Further down the list, the earnings of the tool sharpeners are considerably higher than those of people in the four jobs immediately above them.

A provisional grade structure for this job population is shown by the numbered rectangles drawn round groups of the dots. The lower horizontal line represents a proposed basic rate for each grade, and the upper horizontal line the hourly earnings figure at standard or target performance. The cost implications of these proposals will be discussed later.

119

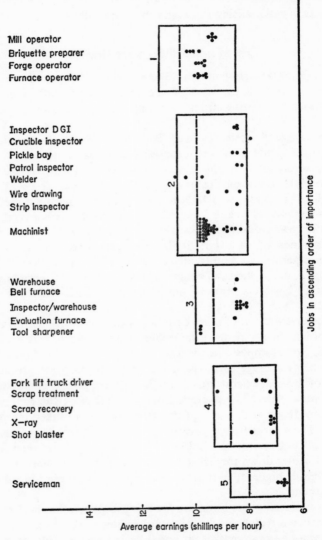

FIGURE 11:1   PROPOSED GRADE STRUCTURE: COMPANY A

First, the implications of the overall grade structure should be considered. It will be seen that the holders of certain jobs—for example, furnace operators, inspectors in all categories, and scrap recovery personnel—benefit greatly from the proposals. Other groups —notably welders, machinists, and particularly tool sharpeners— would receive a good deal less.

So far an important variable has not been mentioned: the current performance levels of the various groups of employees. The significance of this factor may be illustrated by taking two groups of employees, furnace operators and forge operators, whom it is proposed to put in the same grade and whose current level of average hourly earnings are the same. Each group has the same target earnings figure—an identical earnings potential. But the two groups will only benefit equally if their current performance levels are identical. Let us assume they are not—that the furnace preparers are already working at standard performance, whereas the forge operators are working what has been assessed as a 75 performance on the British Standard 75–100 scale (where 100 represents standard performance).

What happens to these two groups if the proposals are implemented? If the furnace operators maintain their current standard of performance, they immediately earn the new target earnings figure for their grade of 11s 6d (£0.57½) an hour—an increase of approximately 1s 6d (7½p) an hour. The forge operators, on the other hand, have to increase their level of performance by 33½ per cent if they are to attain a similar level of earnings. In fact, they can obtain an increase of 15 per cent in average hourly earnings, but only if their performance is increased by 33½ per cent. They benefit less from the proposals, but the structure has been made more equitable, since the holders of similar jobs are paid the same for similar levels of performance.

This complex interrelationship of current performance and earnings levels with revised grade structure proposals will have to be considered when a wages structure is rationalised. Such factors determine the cost of implementation and the financial benefits that will accrue. But before they are considered in more detail, other implications of grade structure proposals should be considered with reference to another illustration.

The scattergram in Figure 11:2 is set out in a form similar to the one already considered. The evidence it provides, however, reveals a different situation. Here the wage structure is much more anomalous than that in Figure 11:1. The spread of earnings for jobs in the same grade is a good deal wider. This indicates loose incentive schemes, an inequitable basic rate structure, and a lack of control which exposes management to strong pressures from employees and their unions. The cost of rationalisation will be high if order is to be introduced into this situation. A provisional grade structure is shown on the scattergram, and two groups of employees may be identified which were not found in the previous example. They are:

1   Employees whose current level of earnings is below the basic rates proposed for the grade to which their job is assigned.
2   Employees whose current level of earnings is above the target level of earnings for the grade to which their job is assigned.

Such groups commonly occur when a wages structure is rationalised. The first group—those earning less than the proposed basic rate for their grade—will benefit, irrespective of their performance level. Under the proposals shown in Figure 11:2 all these employees, whatever their performance, would be paid at least the basic rate for the grade. They would receive an immediate increase when the new structure was implemented, and the total amount of the increases would be a cost the company would have to pay for rationalisation. So here is one clearly identifiable cost of rationalising a wages structure.

The calculation of the theoretical cost is more complex. It is the total increase in its wage bill which the company would be faced with if there were no change in employees' performance levels. The actual figure is not easy to obtain, as it means identifying not only the current and proposed earnings level of every individual concerned but also his current level of actual performance. The latter may not sound difficult to obtain, but in our experience the stated levels of individual performance which determine incentive payments under payment-by-results systems rarely bear any relationship to objective standards.

The second group of employees—those currently earning above the target earnings figure for their grade—are overpaid; they are anomalies for whom a policy must be determined. (The only exception would be if their current levels of performance were above standard performance in the same proportion that their current earnings were

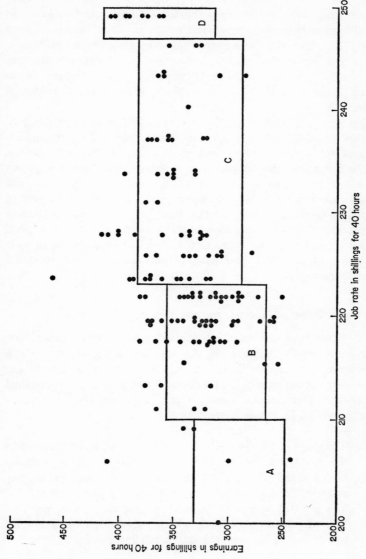

FIGURE 11:2 PROPOSED GRADE STRUCTURE: COMPANY *B*

above the target earnings figure.) Methods of dealing with such anomalies vary. In some cases, the discrepancy is corrected by "buying out" the over-payment through a lump sum calculated on the difference between current and target earnings over an agreed period. Alternatively, these individuals may be given a "protection of earnings" allowance which guarantees their present rates, but provides for absorption of the discrepancy over the years, as increases to the remaining employees raise the level of earnings in each grade.

The examples shown in Figures 11:1–2 illustrate the kind of problem to which solutions must be found. When the cost implications of the various alternatives are accurately assessed, realistic negotiation about the options can be entered into, and companies will know with some accuracy what they and their employees will obtain if the agreement is implemented. In view of the significance of the whole exercise, it is important that the costs of rationalisation be determined as accurately as possible. Ultimately, they will depend on the type of wage structure established, the proportions of base rate and bonus, and the relationship of increases in bonus to increases in performance.

Effect of incentive payments on company costs

The full cost implications of introducing a new wages structure are most conveniently illustrated by the case of a wage structure which incorporates a "variable," or incentive, element based on time saved. In any incentive system based on the time saved by operators against a standard performance target, there are three inter-dependent variables which fix bonus curves:

1   The share of the savings in hours worked which is allocated to the work-force or operator. This determines the slope of the bonus line, which gives the percentage increase in pay awarded for a given percentage increase in performance.
2   The level of output to be achieved for target performance.
3   The target earnings level, which sets the pay rate for all performances between the minimum and the maximum.

By way of illustration, the bonus curves in Figure 11:3 have been drawn for shares of savings equal to one third, a half, three-quarters and all (1) the labour cost savings measured by time saved. From these curves it can be seen that, as the share apportioned to the work-force is increased, the bonus paid for its current performance is decreased. At the same time the incentive element of employee's pay (the slope of the bonus curve) increases. When the same pay system is to be applied to a wide spread of current earnings, the problem is to combine a sufficiently high degree of incentive with an initial bonus high enough to rationalise the pay structure effectively.

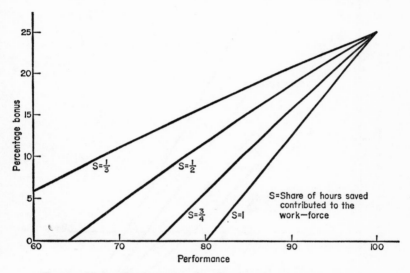

FIGURE 11:3   COMPARISON OF EFFECTS ON BONUS CURVES OF
DIFFERENT SHARES FOR TIME-SAVED SCHEMES

As the average performance of the work-force increases, the company will be paying higher individual wages to fewer people, with an overall reduction in the wage bill. The rate at which the wage bill shrinks will increase with the company's share of the time saved. At the same time, the installation cost will increase because the performance–bonus curve becomes progressively less steep. For a given target earnings level, the two extremes are direct piecework and high day rate. Under the former system, the company's share of time saved is realised only from the initially overpaid people; the bonus line is steep and the installation costs are low. If the target earnings are paid immediately as a high-day rate, the installation costs will

125

be high, but the unit cost of labour will fall rapidly if performance increases. There is, however, no financial incentive to assist management in obtaining this increase in performance. The gross value of a company's savings at the target performance levels will not be affected, since these savings depend only on the increases in earnings and performance at the target levels.

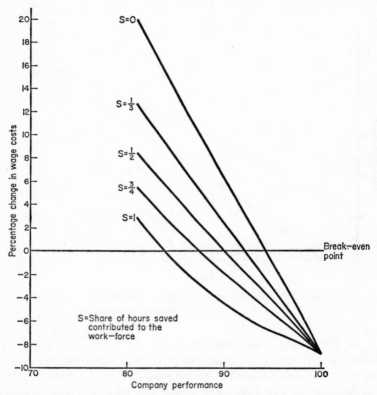

FIGURE 11:4   ACTUAL EXAMPLE OF VARIATIONS IN WAGE COSTS ACCORDING TO THE SHARE OF LABOUR COSTS SAVINGS ALLOCATED TO THE WORK FORCE

The effect of reducing the share of savings to the work-force is to increase its starting bonus level and to reduce the incentive element in the scheme. The curves in Figure 11:4 show the effects for a particular company. Savings are plotted against performance for shares of savings to the work-force at 0, $\frac{1}{3}$, $\frac{1}{2}$, $\frac{3}{4}$ and 1. The installation costs become progressively lower as the slope of the bonus curve steepens. At the same time, the scheme becomes less attractive by virtue of the corresponding fall in the starting bonus levels.

Companies can, therefore, choose from a range of options when rationalising their wage structures. The existing pattern of earnings, the type of variable element proposed, the views of management and employees about how rationalisation should be accomplished and the share of savings to each—all will affect the final decision and the cost implications. What we have tried to show is that the cost implications of the various options can be determined, and will in themselves contribute to what is finally agreed.

Part IV
INSTALLATION OF A PRODUCTIVITY AGREEMENT

12	*Devising the Agreement*	131
13	*Manpower Planning and Security of Employment*	144
14	*Communications*	151
15	*Negotiation and Implementation*	163

Twelve

Devising the Agreement

Preceding chapters have examined the principles on which an equitable wage structure should be based. In most cases, rationalisation should be implemented within the context of a comprehensive productivity agreement. There are three reasons:

1   Rationalising wage structures can be costly (up to 12 per cent of the annual wage bill may be involved). However, the costs are generally balanced by the greater productivity which improved incentive systems can release.

2   Changes in the wage structure have a significant impact on other aspects of employee utilisation such as labour flexibility, job enlargement, overtime levels and so on. Such changes must be probed and discussed when the detailed agreement is being developed with employees' participation.

3   A company should relate changes in the financial motivation of its employees to the total motivational environment it wishes to establish. Payment systems reflect the values of the company and its management. When these are re-examined and the wage structure changed complementary changes are often necessary.

What sort of changes have productivity agreements sought to bring about? Examination of agreements that have been widely publicised will reveal many of the following features:

1   A drastic reduction in the amount of overtime working.

2   A revision of working hours, including the introduction or amendment of shift rotas.

131

3   Enhanced flexibility of labour, job enlargement and the removal of demarcation lines.
4   The introduction of work study or other productivity measurement criteria.
5   Staff status and fringe benefits.
6   A security-of-employment plan incorporating redundancy provisions and safeguards.

The last aspect will be considered in Chapter 13, since in our view a security-of-employment plan is essential to an effective productivity deal. The most significant of the remaining features are discussed below.

Case for reducing overtime

The early productivity agreements, which were negotiated in process control industries, laid heavy stress on large-scale reductions in overtime levels. In many cases this reduction in overtime was considered the most important result of the agreement. In British industry, overtime has been running at a high level for most of the post-war period. Despite the various reductions in the standard working week, the actual hours worked have changed little since 1938, remaining in the region of 46–48 hours a week.

Until recently, this level of overtime was regarded as a major problem of effective labour utilisation. "The overtime blight" was the phrase used to describe it, and production managers were quoted as saying that they were completely dominated by the need to provide employees with regular overtime. Thus there was great interest in the productivity agreement negotiated at the Esso Petroleum Company's Fawley refinery, which set out to reduce overtime from an average of 18 per cent to about two per cent. In order to achieve this the company offered a massive increase in wage rates.

A slightly later agreement negotiated by the Mobil Oil Company Limited at its Coryton refinery centred on an interesting approach to the overtime issue. Before the signing of the agreement, average overtime was in the region of seven hours a week. Very soon afterwards, overtime among the 880 employees had virtually disappeared. Of great significance was the provision that any overtime necessary would be paid for only by time off in lieu. A short time after the agreement was signed, there was a serious fire at the refinery. Repairs had to be carried out quickly, and a period of intensive work beyond normal working hours was required of many employees. The management suggested to the shop stewards' committee that special overtime payments should be made during this emergency period. The committee felt that this would create a precedent which could be embarrassing both to the company and to the shop stewards, so it was decided to abide by the agreement, and no money payment was made for the overtime.

These and other examples revealed that companies could achieve a substantial reduction in labour costs by drastically curtailing overtime. How universal is this situation in British industry? Why does systematic overtime continue? What are managements' and employees' attitudes to overtime?

In many industries the premium payments for overtime are relatively low. They are related to basic rates which are negotiated at national level, and such rates may be only 50 per cent of the average hourly rate of pay. The latter is enhanced by lieu bonuses or piecework earnings. Thus although overtime premiums may appear to be reasonably high, varying from 20 to 40 per cent for weekday overtime to a premium of 100 per cent for Sunday work, appearances are deceptive. Weekend overtime is certainly costly, but this is often not true of overtime worked in the evening. A simple example will suffice. A company pays a particular group of employees £22 per forty-hour week, or 11s (55p) an hour. This level of pay is made up of a £12 basic rate, on which premiums such as overtime and shifts are calculated, and a £10 lieu bonus. The overtime premium is 33⅓ per cent for weekdays. Thus an employee earns 11s (55p) an hour for the first 40 hours worked in a week, and for subsequent hours 13s (65p) an hour. This is made up as follows:

Basic rate:	6s (30p) an hour
Lieu bonus:	5s (25p) an hour
Overtime rate (one-third of basic rate):	2s (10p) an hour
Total:	13s (65p) an hour

This is an additional wage cost to the company of 18 per cent for overtime hours.

This may at first sight appear high. But compare it with the cost of not working overtime and recruiting additional labour instead. The additional employees will be paid, in our example, at 11s (55p) an hour—at least when they become proficient. While they may be paid lower rates until they achieve proficiency, the company is incurring training costs and getting less in the way of production. In addition the company incurs other continuous charges in taking on additional employees—national insurance contributions, graduated and/or company pension contributions, and so on. Moreover, it has taken on a permanent resource which must be fully utilised. Overtime is essential to cope with short-term pressures.

Thus overtime is not necessarily expensive in terms of costs when compared with alternatives such as taking on additional employees. More important is the effect of regular overtime on productivity levels and employees' attitudes. Overtime becomes systematic and passes out of managerial control when companies' wage structures and payment levels fail to provide employees with adequate take-home pay for forty hours' work. Enmeshed by national agreements whose rates of pay bear little relation to employees' required earnings levels or to local market rates, managements assist in creating overtime opportunities so as to attract and retain employees of the necessary calibre. For their part, employees do their best to ensure that regular overtime continues by regulating their pace of work. In the last resort, employees may threaten industrial action if overtime is jeopardised.

Paradoxically, employees also use overtime bans to exert pressure on employers. This is effective where overtime has become so institutionalised that it is regarded as normal by management and employees. Production schedules or service requirements—for example, maintenance—are met through regular overtime and generally forty-hour earnings are lower for indirect workers than for those on production work. It is frequently found in analysing the earnings levels of all a company's employees over a reference period that time workers' hours include more overtime than do those of the people on incentive schemes. This situation allows time workers to attain a reasonable level of take-home pay, while management, conscious of the need to retain employees, gives way to their pressure for regular overtime.

Other things being equal, productivity levels suffer when regular overtime is worked. Employees pace themselves when they know they will be working a nine or ten hour day. Perhaps more important, they feel that overtime—however systematic—may suddenly be cut back, and so they take all steps necessary to ensure its continuation. Those on direct incentives often control their immediate environment to a remarkable degree—manipulating the incentive system to provide reasonable bonus levels, and at the same time ensuring that jobs are not completed quickly enough to jeopardise overtime. Such control occurs even where measurement standards are reasonably accurate.

In many companies, overtime is necessary to meet urgent delivery dates, sudden upswings in production schedules, or to give management a degree of flexibility in matching labour capacity to production demands. There is some evidence that employees are naturally inclined to work for something over forty hours a week, and may not see great benefits in any substantial reduction of the working week. Changes that give employees' more leisure should perhaps be "sold" more on the basis of longer holidays or earlier retirement. Unions are less likely to press for these while reductions in the working week remain one of the most effective means of increasing their members' earnings levels.

One may conclude that in the majority of cases productivity agreements should make provision for a reduction in overtime. When realistic earnings levels are negotiated at plant level, the pressure for overtime will be reduced. Most companies will need to work overtime, particularly where day work or alternating day and night shifts are established, to meet changes in the pattern of demand. Provided overtime remains under management control and is used for this purpose, it is clearly desirable. On the other hand, systematic overtime should be avoided, and a properly devised productivity deal will ensure that there is no need for it to make up employees' take-home pay. Management will then be in a position to control employees' hours of work.

Revision of working hours

The majority of productivity agreements have provided for the revision of working hours and the introduction of, or revisions to, shift work. Different shift and rota systems are provided for, and in some cases employees are asked to accept new hours of work after a stipulated period of notice or consultation. For example, the industry-wide agreement negotiated by the electricity supply industry provided for staggered day working, staggered working hours to meet the need for weekend maintenance, and other changes of a similar nature. In return, employees were paid compensatory weekly or annual allowances and premium payments for weekend work. In the widely publicised agreement negotiated by the Tubes Limited subsidiary of Tube Investments Limited, the following provisions were made for changes to existing hours of work:

1   The abolition of permanent night shifts.
2   The establishment of the following shift rotas:
    (a) Alternating day and night shift system.
    (b) Rotating 3 shift system (non-continuous).
    (c) Rotating 3 shift system (continuous).

Not all agreements provide for the introduction of shift work. On the contrary, Mobil's Coryton agreement discontinued permanent shift work for maintenance workers, who were transferred to day work. They received *ex gratia* payments. Similar provisions were included in an agreement concluded by Alcan Industries Limited. The number of employees on shifts was greatly reduced, and those taken off shift work received *ex gratia* payments of as much as £110.

Such cases tend to be exceptional. In 1967 the then Minister of Labour (Mr R Gunter) stated in a foreword to a Ministry booklet [*Introduction to Shift Working*] on shiftwork that: "The number of manual workers engaged on shift work has grown by more than half during the last decade." The booklet reported the results of a survey of nineteen firms, employing 30 000 employees, which had introduced, or attempted to introduce, shift work. Four main reasons were given by the companies for introducing shift systems:

1 Greater use of expensive plant and machinery
Shift work produces not only higher levels of production but also an improved return on the generally large amounts of capital invested.

2 Reduction in overtime
A third of the firms in the survey sought to reduce excessively high overtime hours through introducing shifts. (This was one of the major aims in the rationalisation of shift systems at Tubes Limited.)

3 Attracting labour
They are used primarily to attract female employees in a tight labour market where part-time or short day shifts may attract women, particularly married women, who cannot work full time. This is unlikely to feature prominently in a productivity agreement, but it

may well result from an intensive analysis of labour turnover and absence levels among female employees.

4 Demands of special processes

In some instances, shift work is necessary to cope with the special demands of manufacturing processes, for example automatic plant which is costly or very inconvenient to close down. Here negotiation would begin when the introduction of such plant was being considered, and it is unlikely to feature as part of a productivity deal.

Thus the introduction of shift work as part of a comprehensive productivity agreement is likely to be due to one or both of the first two factors listed above. Each case requires detailed analysis in the light of the particular circumstances of the company. Certain general conclusions can be drawn, however. In the first place, the cost implications of introducing shift work must be analysed carefully. The increased production available from shift work is of fundamental importance and, of course, has to be sold. These expected extra sales must be reasonably steady, not liable to rapid short term fluctuations. Double day and rotating three-shift systems, being relatively inflexible, do not permit major changes in the gross labour man-hours worked. If a company needs flexibility in this respect because of fluctuating market demand, shifts, where introduced, should facilitate overtime working to absorb short term production peaks. In the Ministry of Labour survey referred to above, most of the companies which had introduced shift work had carried out a thorough cost investigation. One firm had found that depreciation as a proportion of total costs had fallen from 44 to 20 per cent and, although labour costs rose from 38 to 52 per cent, unit costs of production fell by about 30 per cent.

Second, the sociological implications of introducing shift work require careful consideration. Employees are concerned with a range of problems shift work creates for them—interference with weekends, seeing their children, taking part in or watching sport, difficulties of early rising, and so on. In localities where shift work is rare, the problems due to the pressures of the neighbourhood can be difficult to overcome. When shift work is introduced in such areas, companies may experience serious recruitment problems or find that labour turnover, lateness and absence are all abnormally high.

Full consultation with employees and a detailed study of these factors are necessary before final decisions are taken. If the decision to introduce shift work is taken as part of a comprehensive productivity deal, it should be recognised that it may prolong negotiations and delay implementation. Such agreements ask employees to accept sweeping changes. In some cases, the introduction of shift work may make demands on employees' capacity to absorb changes that are too heavy. In others, it may be accepted more readily as part of an overall agreement which offers substantial financed benefits—benefits which can be enhanced by attractive shift premiums. Each case must depend on the particular company and regional position, but each requires accurate information on which management decisions may be based.

Labour flexibility

Job enlargement and restrictive practices

This is another aspect of classical productivity agreements whose significance has been overstressed as far as the greater part of British industry is concerned. The impression has arisen that restrictive practices (or "protective practices" as employees regard them) are the major reason for low labour productivity. [See, for example, the speech of Harold Wilson, to the TUC, 5 September 1966. The greatest contribution which the trade union movement could make to increased productivity is "the elimination of every avoidable restrictive practice."] This is an exaggeration. Serious over-manning from such restrictions is largely confined to a handful of industries, notably shipbuilding, printing, and the docks.

It certainly existed in the oil industry but has largely disappeared following the negotiation of a number of agreements by major oil companies in the wake of Esso's Fawley scheme.

A number of sweeping criticisms of the extent and effect of restrictive practices in British industry have recently been published. [See, for example, G Jones and M Barnes, *Britain on Borrowed Time*, Penguin Books.] In some industries, especially printing and the docks, the balance of industrial power appears to have been almost completely reversed: unions and employees exhibit a rigidity and conservatism which threatens their long-term interests. They manifest attitudes they are quick to condemn in employers; managements are faced with an enormous task if industrial relations are to be restructured or basic changes in attitude achieved.

138

Yet in another industry traditionally subject to the problems of widespread restrictive practices, shipbuilding, changes of this sort are slowly being won. The pacemaker in introducing them, Fairfield's, lost its momentum when it was merged with other Clyde shipyards and several of the most dynamic members of senior management left. However, the "Fairfield experiment"[1] gained sufficient drive to make the industry sit up and take notice. Greater security, more stable pay packets, effective consultation and a problem-solving approach to areas of conflict were shown to have an effect upon the shipyard worker and the industry's industrial relations. Though many restrictions remain, there has been an improvement, and already shipyards on the Tyne, the Clyde, and the Wear have succeeded in negotiating greater flexibility across, for example, the boiler-making trades, in return for imaginative proposals designed to give shipyard workers greater security.

In these and industries with similar problems, productivity agreements will centre on the removal of labour restrictions. In others, such as the chemical industry and in some areas engineering, a blurring of demarcations between the skilled craftsmen and higher grade production or process workers may be sought, together with the removal of limitations on promotion to skilled grades.

Such changes may certainly help to increase productivity, but in most industries they are of secondary importance. The idea that restrictive practices are a nation-wide problem, which was created largely by the publicity given to the early productivity agreements, is untrue. Where such restrictions do exist, they are most frequently the product of badly designed wage structures which establish numerous differentials between similar levels of work, or of individual incentive schemes which encourage employees to regard their jobs as personal property.

The introduction of rationalised and equitable wage structures will do much to remove these limitations on labour flexibility and permit the introduction of job enlargement programmes. Such programmes provide training for employees over a range of jobs in a similar grade as the production processes of the particular plant allow. The extent of a company's need for such flexibility is a significant determinant of the number of grades established in a revised wage structure. Broadly, the greater the need for the flexible use of employees across a range of similar jobs, the fewer the grades in the structure.

[1] See: Paulden and Hawkins, *Whatever Happened at Fairfields?* Gower Press, 35s. (£1.75).

Similarly the design of the variable or incentive element in the wages structure will also affect the ease with which management obtains flexibility from its work-force. The writers have worked with some companies to replace individual or small group incentive schemes by large group bonuses determined by plant measures of performance based on the overall output per man-hour worked. In such cases, the pay of all operators in the plant is determined by their grade rate and the overall performance level of the operators. The following example from a tube mill shows the effect of such a group incentive on flexibility requirements as the basis by which the bonus is determined.

The operators were organised in working groups of up to twelve people and trained to become proficient in several departmental tasks. They were expected to transfer from task to task as the mix and flow of work changed. If such transfers required operators to work in a higher-paid job, the higher grade rate was paid while this job was undertaken. Output levels were maintained by training all operators to work their plant or machinery effectively at the optimum speeds.

The bonus was designed to operate so that half the value of every working hour saved was shared between the operators and management. If the same amount of output was produced by fewer operators, half the value of the hours saved was available for distribution among employees. If output increased with the same work-force, the value of the standard hours equivalent to increased output was shared in the same way. Thus the scheme encouraged each employee to work his particular machine at the optimum rate and to ensure that as much of his time as possible was spent on productive work.

The implications of this system for increased labour flexibility and job enlargement are clear: managers and foremen have to take advantage of the opportunities provided and will be under pressure from employees to do so. It should be noted that among the advantages of such a system of payment is the greater intrinsic job interest it offers to employees who are asked to undertake a wider range of work than before.

Reactions to work study

In some parts of the country, employees and unions are highly suspicious of work study. This suspicion is directed primarily towards work measurement, and in these cases the stop-watch becomes a symbol of oppression; its appearance on the shop floor can lead to an immediate walk-out. This apprehension of work measurement has strong emotional overtones, but it is based on fundamentally rational misgivings which can be broadly classified into two: (a) fears of redundancy and (b) loss of bargaining power. These are, in our experience, much more important than opposition to the enhanced effort employees may be required, or feel they may be asked, to give under work-measured schemes. This is not to say that there are no fears about "sweated labour"—only that they are less important than other misgivings.

Fear that work study will lead to redundancy is found primarily in those parts of the country where unemployment is highest, notably Scotland and the North-East of England. Here the "efficiency expert," the "time and motion" study man, has become part of working class mythology, a feared instrument of oppressive bosses who seek to condemn the worker to an exhausting pace of work and create wholesale redundancies.

In other areas, notably the prosperous Midlands, employees' opposition centres on the knowledge that it will reduce their very considerable bargaining power. Piecework schemes are in operation all over the country under which individual negotiation between the employee and the rate fixer determines the "stint"—the amount of work (measured physically or by time) which will be allowed for the agreed bonus rate; but they are particularly common in the Midlands.

Government policies designed to encourage more accurate measurement of productivity ("the application of proper work standards") are having an effect upon the continued existence of subjectively based measurement. Where more objective criteria are introduced and accepted, standards of performance can be largely removed from negotiation, which will then be concerned with the payment levels for a given performance. The latter rightly become the centre of negotiation between management and employees. Every effort should be made to ensure that performance standards remain as objective as possible. Management should take as much time and trouble as necessary to demonstrate the accuracy and fairness of the standards to their employees. This is essential if reasonable control of wage costs is to be maintained and some semblance of order in the industrial relations situation established. Nothing creates an environment of conflict and dispute more readily than daily bargaining about standards on the shop floor.

With the increasing use of synthetic predetermined measurement standards which, like MTM for example, have been validated internationally, and the introduction of rational payment structures giving stability of earnings and equitable differentials, a real opportunity exists to gain employees' acceptance of work study as an objective and helpful measurement tool—not a weapon of control to be inflicted on them.

Regulation of lateness and absenteeism

In an article called "Stay-at-home Britain" a leading management journal [*British Industry Week*, 26 January 1968] stated that "Every day over a million people—up to five per cent of Britain's labour force—are absent from work." While about 75 per cent of this total are sick, the remainder—a substantial proportion—just stay at home. The article went on to describe the methods a number of concerns, including the National Coal Board, are using to try to overcome the problem. Many were using financial incentives in various forms, or other material rewards such as prizes.

If a company has a serious absence or lateness problem, it is certainly worth considering finding a solution within the framework of a productivity agreement. No solution is likely to be found if the company merely defines new standards of attendance and attempts to incorporate them in the agreement. Even if formal agreement is obtained, conflict is merely being stored up for the future.

If, however, the agreement can obtain employees' and trade unions' participation in defining attendance standards, and their involvement in ensuring that these standards are met, then a real change for the better may be established. Trade unions are wont to say that they are seeking a "joint regulation of the employment situation." This question of attendance is an area where such joint regulation can be established.

The Firestone Tyre and Rubber Company, with its joint disciplinary committee and others, have proved that with mature trade union representatives the constructive involvement of employees can be obtained in areas which directly concern them.

Staff status and fringe benefits

Experience suggests that questions of full staff status and fringe benefits are of secondary importance to most employees. Some unnecessary distinctions between staff and works employees *do* irritate and should be examined, primarily because they reflect so clearly management's philosophy (or lack of it) towards manual workers.

Such examination often reveals an unexpected situation. In some respects, the manual worker enjoys *better* conditions than the office employee. Age scales, for example, finish earlier for the fitter than for the draughtsman; overtime premiums are generally higher, and in some instances manual workers enjoy better holiday entitlements, overall, than staff employees—who may have to put in years of service before they get more than two weeks' holiday.

Staff employees certainly have better fringe benefits in most cases, notably in the case of sickness and pension provisions. However, the improvement in national social security provisions has reduced the extent of this advantage. Attitude surveys and discussions with employees show that they regard improvements in sickness and pension arrangements as deferred benefits; given the choice, they prefer improvements in the form of pay increases, the benefits of which they experience more quickly and more directly.

We have described some of the principal components of productivity agreements and suggested that their relevance to increased productivity and improved relations may have been over-stressed. When a productivity agreement is created around a major rationalisation of the wages structure, the decisions on earnings levels, share of the savings, type of incentive payments, and so on, will largely determine the changes proposed in overtime levels, increased flexibility and measurement standards. Major changes in working hours may be an important component of the agreement, but they involve a change in employees' lives which may provoke continued resistance. The possibility must be weighed against the prospective benefits.

When considering the allocation of the employees' share of the savings from a productivity deal, shop stewards will, if they have the option, generally seek higher earnings rather than better fringe benefits. Companies have an educational job to do here in getting employees to look beyond their short-term interests. They should do this within a long term policy framework designed to remove unnecessary anomalies in employment conditions between the various grades of employee.

_____ *Thirteen* _____

Manpower Planning
and Security of Employment

Most attitude surveys the writers have carried out have confirmed
the importance of job security to employees. In many cases it has
been their principal requirement (see Chapter 6). The negotiation
of a comprehensive productivity deal brings this issue to the fore-
front, and a carefully designed plan defining the company's policy
is an essential component of any worthwhile agreement. Such a plan
is not (or should not) be a "no redundancy," guarantee. Even if such
a guarantee were possible in the short term, it evades the issue and is
likely to encourage both management and unions to sweep this
important but difficult question under the carpet.

In fact, relatively few companies can honestly give a guarantee of
"no redundancy" in relation to a comprehensive productivity agreement. The range of potential increases in productivity in most firms
is a 15–50 per cent improvement, with 25–30 per cent as the mean.
Few companies can guarantee to sell the 25 per cent more output
their employees will produce when the productivity agreement has
been implemented. If the extra output cannot be sold, companies
may not be able to absorb higher productivity by reducing the gross
man-hours worked through natural wastage or reductions in overtime. If these measures—increased sales, normal wastage or overtime
reduction—cannot absorb the productivity increase, manpower
levels must be reduced by other means.

The issue of redundancy should not be evaded. On the other
hand, it must be put in perspective. In many parts of the country,

144

redundancy is beginning to lose its emotive connotations; the Contracts of Employment Act and the Redundancy Payments Act are having their effect. What employees are really concerned about is that management should never return to the "bad old days" of hire-and-fire, but should treat any possibility of having to terminate employment with the care and attention its significance warrants. There are two sides to this care and attention. One is taking all reasonable steps to ensure continuity of employment—that is, manpower planning—and the other is making imaginative, effective provisions when continuity of employment is threatened. Both aspects are closely related but, in the interests of clarity, they will be considered separately in this chapter.

Economic necessity for manpower planning

The Institute of Personnel Management has defined manpower planning as ". . . the setting of manpower targets based on the construction of long- and short-term company objectives, founded on variables which are always changing; thus frequent reconstruction is needed. The plan should be not only in quantitive terms but also in qualitative terms (e.g. state of training). As changing economic and organisational conditions occur, company conditions will change and thus influence changes in manpower plans."

The sort of productivity agreement we are concerned with here is a good example of the changing conditions which affect manpower plans. The purpose of manpower planning is to safeguard, as economically as possible, the company's future manpower needs by developing and implementing plans which satisfy those requirements. Manpower planning is not solely, nor even predominantly, justifiable as a means of satisfying employees' job security needs. Its major justification must lie in its economic return. Manpower is a primary resource of, and a major cost to, the great majority of companies, and a properly devised plan is of material assistance in satisfying a company's requirements and of controlling elements of its labour costs. These aspects lie outside the scope of this book, as does any detailed consideration of the techniques which have been developed to improve the accuracy of manpower planning.

Two points are relevant in the context of security of employment and productivity bargaining. First, a company which, in developing a productivity agreement, undertakes to take account of employees' security needs cannot meet its undertaking honestly unless it plans its manpower needs.

Second, the sort of comprehensive agreement we have described will often transform employees' opinion of the company and ultimately its reputation in the locality as well. Firms whose employees have always given below-average performance in return for earnings made up only by long hours of overtime can restructure their working environment, performance levels and earnings opportunities through a comprehensive productivity agreement. Hours may be reduced but two- or three-shift working may feature in the agreement's proposals. The industrial and human relations environment may alter radically.

Changes like these which change the company's image as an employer—can produce, among other things, a major impact on labour turnover. Difficulties may be experienced in such a situation when a company begins manpower planning and develops predictive methods of forecasting its natural wastage, using statistical data. The predictions may prove totally inaccurate for the period following implementation of a productivity agreement. Some companies have found turnover to be substantially reduced after introducing such agreements. Caution should therefore be exercised in assessing the contribution of natural wastage towards reducing the number of gross man-hours worked so as to absorb productivity increases.

For both management and employees, manpower planning is therefore a long term need. The period of radical change following the negotiation of an agreement may completely alter the company's manpower needs and the level of natural wastage. Usually the situation will eventually stabilise and more accurate planning will be possible. But because there is a period of uncertainty among management and employees when a productivity agreement is implemented, a detailed security-of-employment plan should take account of it.

Developing a security-of-employment plan

There are therefore short- and long-term considerations in developing a security-of-employment plan as an integral part of a productivity agreement. In the long term, management should establish, in collaboration with employees' representatives, a detailed policy laying down the means by which security of employment will be sought, and the procedures to be followed if unforeseen events make reductions in manpower or hours of work unavoidable. In the short term, special measures may be required if the potential increases in productivity are to be attained.

The longer-term considerations are the more fundamental and will be considered first. A security of employment plan has three primary objectives:

1   To obviate the need for redundancy whenever possible by taking alternative measures to achieve the requisite reduction in gross man-hours worked.

2   To minimise the hardship, financial and otherwise, suffered by employees who through no fault of their own are asked to terminate their employment.

3   To develop employees' morale and co-operation by demonstrating, in a practical manner, the company's concern with security of employment. By so doing, management explicitly recognises that security is one of employees' prime needs.

We have included a detailed example of a security-of-employment plan in Appendix 6. This sets out the means by which redundancy will be avoided if possible and, where this fails, redundancy criteria, periods of warning and notice, and the basis on which compensation will be paid. The plan also provides for an appeals procedure and personal safeguards if redundancy has to be declared. Its provisions are consistent with, and complementary to, the provisions of the Contracts of Employment Act and Redundancy Payments Act.

Certain aspects should be particularly stressed. First, the plan sets out the measures the company will take to avoid redundancy when there is a surplus of manpower. The cessation of recruitment, internal transfers, the reduction of overtime and introduction of short-time working are to be considered and put into effect whenever practicable. Redundancy is a last resort.

Where these measures prove inadequate, the redundancy policy is comprehensive. It has the following features:

1   It provides as long a period of warning as possible.

2   It does not differentiate between different categories of employee.

3   It establishes dismissal criteria which are seen to be fair and which meet all reasonable requirements of management.

147

4   Employees are compensated for goodwill and length of service by payments additional to those demanded by law.

5   It reduces hardship by providing a measure of financial assistance to redundant employees who experience difficulty in obtaining other suitable work.

6   The company gives redundant employees active help in finding other suitable employment.

7   The plan covers all situations in which redundancy may be necessitated, and provides for full consultation with employees' representatives as soon as the possibility is foreseen.

This security-of-employment plan is offered as a model, but is not necessarily applicable universally. Each case must be determined by the situation, by tradition, by the attitude of the company and by the needs and requirements of its employees. We submit, however, that it gives a clear idea of the aspects a plan should cover and of the possible scale of benefits.

The possible need for special provisions to cover redundancy in the short term has already been mentioned. Consider, for example, the case of a company which can increase productivity by 25 per cent in a year through a productivity deal, but which is faced with a static order book. Demand will not improve immediately through any slight reduction in selling price. The labour turnover figure is 10 per cent. It will be necessary to consider specific measures to deal with this situation if a realistic agreement is to be implemented. In this instance, employees remaining with the company will benefit from the increased earnings opportunities the agreement proposes— provided that a limited number of their colleagues are prepared to leave. So it is in the interests of both management and trade unions to negotiate generous termination payments for voluntary leavers.

Such redundancy could become a major obstacle to the successful negotiation of the agreement. But if the unions are offered financial protection for members who leave the company, and if the redundancy is established on a voluntary basis, their agreement may be obtained. The voluntary aspect should be emphasised. If management attempts to enforce redundancy, specifying the people it no longer requires, the chances of the agreement being accepted are dim. Employees' loyalty to their colleagues is generally, and rightly, strong. The majority are unlikely to accept the agreement if it means explicitly discarding a minority of their number. A generous voluntary redundancy procedure is another matter.

Such a process may have to be carefully structured from management's point of view. An ill defined voluntary procedure might lead to the company's losing many of its best employees, or a majority from a certain age group, which would upset the age distribution among its work-force. These factors should be discussed with shop stewards. When such an imbalance seems likely with a general voluntary redundancy, management and shop stewards should work out a scale of payments that encourages the employees the company can afford to lose to leave of their own free will. In one company where voluntary redundancy was necessary for implementing a productivity agreement, the age distribution of the work-force was already out of balance. There was a predominance of men over 45, among whom were a number with relatively short service. They had been recruited during the past five years, when the local labour market was very tight, and were generally below average calibre.

It was therefore proposed to offer payments beyond those provided under the Redundancy Payments Act to employees who volunteered to leave. The scale proposed was as follows:

> Employees aged 21–30: an additional five weeks' pay.
> Employees aged 31–40: an additional ten weeks' pay.
> Employees aged 41–50: an additional fifteen weeks' pay.
> Employees aged 51–64: an additional twenty weeks' pay.

Thus the older employees were encouraged to leave. Management would have preferred to make no additional payments to employees under thirty, since it wished to retain them, but agreed at the unions' request. After long discussions with the shop stewards, it did obtain some limitation on the application of this scheme. It was not applied to certain designated sections and grades of employees who were highly skilled or who had acquired important company skills which the firm could not afford to lose.

The scheme applied only for the time the productivity agreement was being implemented, to cope with the exceptional circumstances this created. It did not form part of the general security-of-employment plan which was prepared as part of the agreement. This plan was similar to that outlined in Appendix 6, except that it did not provide for payments additional to those required by law, apart from employees with very long service.

In this chapter, we have stressed the importance of establishing a security-of-employment plan as an integral part of the productivity agreement. Such a plan may include short term provisions to deal with the immediate situation caused by the implementation of the agreement, as well as comprehensive long-term proposals which are an integral part of the company's manpower planning. With the increasing rate of technological change, employees will have to be more mobile both within a company and in moving between companies.

Fourteen

Communications

There are two main systems through which a management's philosophy expresses itself: the wages system and the communications system. Communications present at least three difficulties for the writer. The first is that the topic is broad and its boundaries ill defined. Second, so much has been written and spoken on the subject recently that there is a danger (in information theory terms) of adding to the noise which tends to obscure the signal. Third—and perhaps most important—reliable data is scarce. There is evidence, for example, that the works councils resulting from the Whitley Committee are ineffective, but not as to why this should be so.

In view of these difficulties we propose to minimise the effect of the first two by concentrating on the aspects which are of particular relevance to our main theme and stating them boldly. It is hoped in this way to make our signal strong, even if distorted. The third difficulty we attempt to deal with by returning to first principles, and designing a system from these.

Principles of industrial communications

At the risk of appearing naive, we suggest that the salient features of communications can be expressed in a few simple statements. These are that:

1   People in industry have, in general, more problems in common than differences.
2   Bringing the different groups together physically is the best way of helping them to attain their objectives.

151

3   An adequate two-way information flow is necessary before the right decisions can be taken.
4   People try to control their immediate environment, often succeed, and are prepared to improve it given the chance.

In less simple terms, our argument is that an effective communication structure is one of the bases of good management, and that it is especially important in industrial relations. Through such a system, company policies, objectives and practices can be made known to employees. Their effect and the employees' reactions, with suggestions for modification, are fed back. Co-operation in the achievement of common, identified objectives is enhanced. Management also requires an appropriate and effective communications network through which to carry out its managerial role, implement plans and ensure that the unit reacts promptly and in a co-ordinated way to changing circumstances.

The use of an effective consultative structure accustoms both managers (including foremen) and work-people to solving problems jointly. This approach is conducive to the acceptance of change, both on the shop-floor and in the office; in addition it often produces a better solution to the problem. If properly utilised, the practice will extend throughout the company so that this mature and effective method of co-operation comes to be second nature not only within the consultative structure, but also in day-to-day working.

It is important to recognise that this does not mean that a manager is no longer free to manage—to give instructions. It is the *style* of management which is improved. Abrupt, dogmatic orders with little discussion or explanation breed a dependent type of subordinate, reluctant to make his own decisions. The discussion of objectives leads to:

1   Commitment to the task once it is accepted as feasible.
2   Easier delegation: a subordinate is aware of his manager's objectives and hence is able to make decisions in his own sphere without constant reference back.
3   Greater job satisfaction and higher performance.

In attempting to design an effective communications system, there are two main considerations: the characteristics of the system itself and the requirements of the system for the purposes it is to serve.

Characteristics of the system

The basis of all good communications and human interaction is face-to-face contact. This is not to suggest that communication is impossible unless people can actually see and talk to each other. What it does mean is that there must be inter-linking between communicating groups. A man's opinion of his managing director, even though he may never come into contact with him, is strongly influenced by the sort of people the manager allows to be foremen or others in closer contact. We suspect that most of the inadequacies of house journals and the like are due to the fact that they are regarded as sufficient in themselves; they are regarded as a substitute for, and not supportive to, an effective system.

The second important factor is that the transmission and receipt of information is a notoriously subjective process. People's motive for communicating is not necessarily connected with the information communicated. They do not receive and take in all they are expected to. In the process there is a bias in (*a*) the selection of what appears to be relevant, (*b*) the interpretation of what is meant and (*c*) its significance for the recipient. The information system, then, should be:

1   *Comprehensive*: allowing all important information to be transmitted to all the relevant groups. (More copies of documents, for example!)
2   *Multi-directional*: allowing for transfer outwards from and inwards towards the organisation centre, and also laterally. (One cannot reply effectively to a loudspeaker.)
3   *Penetrative*: not stopping short of the periphery of the groups. (Slips in pay packets as well as on notice boards.)
4   *Multi-channelled*: so that the same message travels by several routes, to prevent distortion and ensure authenticity. (The foreman as well as the shop steward.)

Against these criteria the normal situation in a unit, whether it be in relation to management via shop steward to shop floor, or within the management structure itself, should be critically examined.

Requirements of the system for the purposes it is to serve

The "Donovan report" (the report of the Royal Commission on Trade Unions and Employers' Federations) recommended a number

153

of points to be considered in ensuring that the management–employee communications system is designed in the way best suited to the purposes it will be expected to serve; specifically:

"Top management must assume full responsibility for developing comprehensive agreements and overall personnel policies. Specifically, boards should undertake a detailed industrial relations appraisal in accordance with paragraph 182:
'In order to promote the orderly and effective regulation of industrial relations within companies and factories, we recommend that the boards of companies review industrial relations within their undertakings. In doing so, they should have the following objectives in mind:

1   To develop, together with trade unions representative of their employees, comprehensive and authoritative collective bargaining machinery to deal at company and/or factory level with the terms and conditions of employment which are settled at these levels.
2   To develop, together with unions representative of their employees, joint procedures for the rapid and equitable settlement of grievances in a manner consistent with the relevant collective agreements.
3   To conclude with unions representative of their employees agreements regulating the position of shop stewards in matters such as: facilities for holding elections; numbers and constituencies; recognition of credentials; facilities to consult and report back to their members; facilities to meet with other stewards; the responsibilities of the chief shop steward (if any); pay while functioning as steward in working hours; day release with pay for training.
4   To conclude agreements covering the handling of redundancy.
5   To adopt effective rules and procedures governing disciplinary matters, including dismissal, with provision for appeals.
6   To ensure joint regular discussion of measures to promote safety at work.' "

If to this list is added:

7   To ensure regular joint discussion of measures to promote increased productivity.

we have the purposes which a comprehensive communications system has to serve. What does this mean in terms of the design of the system?

Design of a communications system

A comprehensive communications structure comprises four parts:

1   A command or line system.
2   A negotiating system.

154

3   A consultation system.
4   An individual appeals system.

Before considering these in detail it is worth examining the overall concept.

One of the fundamental problems of industrial relations is that of dealing with conflict. There is a tendency to alternate between the two extremes of trying, on the one hand, to eliminate it altogether and, on the other, of allowing it to become all-pervading. The plain fact is that conflict is as inherent in industrial life as anywhere else. There always will be conflict, for example, about the distribution of a unit's revenue. It is interesting to note that even in countries subject to central planning, such as Czechoslovakia, in those units which are at all individually accountable there are also discussions or negotiations about the distribution of surplus that will go into investments, into increased pay or to the State.

What is required, therefore, is a careful distinction between group objectives which are necessarily conflicting and those which are common—in simple terms, those concerned with the *share* of the cake and those concerned with the *size* of the cake. The idea that there can and should be two parallel systems, one concerned with areas of conflict and the other with areas of co-operation is not supported by many trade union officials or even managers.

The trade unions can put forward many arguments against the proposition. The three most important are:

1   It is impossible to decide beforehand whether an item under discussion is negotiable or not. The extreme version of this view is, of course, that *all* items are negotiable.
2   If the same people are to meet to discuss matters, they might as well meet on the same occasion and save time. The implication is that if they are not the same people, some of the representatives may not be shop stewards, and so the unions could not recognise them.
3   There are very few examples of purely consultative systems which are effective.

This rejection of the tea-and-toilets type of consultation is of course one of the main objections of management. It is worth noting, too, that some companies where consultation and negotiation were separated in the past have recently combined the two systems, for example the Samuel Fox and Company branch of the former United Steel Companies, in Sheffield.

To such criticisms one can only reply that past situations were structured by past systems. If we are to change the system it ought to be possible to change the situation. Specifically, each point might be answered along these lines:

1 It is precisely *because* few attempts have been made to separate areas of conflict and co-operation that conflict has spread into all areas. When the attempt has been made, tremendous progress has resulted. Trade union interests are safeguarded in such ways as having the senior shop stewards as *ex officio* members of the works council. They can then decide at any point whether the matter is a fit subject for negotiation.

2 Effective communication requires many more communicators than there are usually shop stewards. The ideal number of constituents per representative is about ten, a practical limit twenty-five to thirty. We are seeking involvement and participation in a very real sense.

3 Consultation systems have usually been purely informative, with a limited range and set in an industrial relations climate which required some means by which employees could reach the management, and *vice versa*. They were usually too large and amorphous to be effective. Much more could be expected from small departmental productivity panels concerned with matters which closely affect members' interests.

The case of Samuel Fox and Company may show what happens in the long run, when active consultation and negotiating systems have existed for some time. But this is not the situation in many companies which require the kind of comprehensive communications structure described below.

Command system

This system is clearly the responsibility of management and is exercised by means of the "chain of command." An effective structure for this function comprises a system of regular "command meetings" at different levels, at which clear objectives are defined, standards of performance and work programmes established and information is received on progress.

This command system should be closely linked with the role specifications. Very little attention is paid to this important system, yet, properly instituted, it is the most effective method of managing. In the industrial relations scene alone, a good deal of unnecessary disturbance arises because foreman and manager are either unable to take a decision through uncertainty of their roles or lack sufficient information.

Neither in the command system nor in the consultation system is management by committee to be recommended. The decisions must come from those responsible for them. In most cases this style of management leads to problem-centred, rather than status-centred, decision taking, produces better results and gives greater job satisfaction. Command meetings should take fifteen to thirty minutes a day.

Negotiating system

Negotiating procedures have been agreed in greater or lesser detail by most employers' associations and by the appropriate unions. They also work to a greater or lesser degree, and have been the subject of much weightier books than this. We do not propose either to summarise or to review what has been said and written.

The negotiating system is concerned with the regulation and resolution of the inevitable conflicts of interest within the organisation. In particular, it is concerned with the terms on which individuals are employed: payment, hours of work and the like. These terms define the boundary separating organisational control from individual control; hence the negotiation function can be regarded as the settlement of "boundary disputes."

These boundary disputes arise as a result of the practices which, in sum, comprise the industrial relations system. If the system is changed, the practices change, and so the requirements are different. A piecework rate-fixing system obviously requires a different kind of structure and negotiating system from a group incentive with an annual improvement factor, operating within a comprehensive agreement. The pressures and disputes will be on a smaller scale and will require much more joint regulation and interpretation of the factors of the agreement.

It is thus feasible to have a joint negotiating committee for most purposes—nearly all, in fact, except in cases like the negotiation of a global increase (whether by means of an added value factor or not) or the problems concerned with renegotiating agreements. Apart from instances like these, the problems are those of applying the terms of the agreement to particular circumstances.

The constitution of the committee will depend upon the circumstances of the unit, the number of unions and the size of the unit. Most situations can be covered by a four-man team, say a works manager, a personnel officer and two senior shop stewards. The committee should meet as required to settle matters which have not been resolved further down the line by the shop stewards and the foremen or, at a further stage, by the departmental manager. Is it too optimistic to envisage a joint committee of this sort exerting a wide range of powers—greater even than those of Firestone's disciplinary committee, which is the final arbiter on, for example, dismissal?

Consultation system

The consultation system is an advisory function dealing with the areas where close co-operation is desirable and possible. It is a process of discussion and joint problem solving, leading usually to jointly agreed action. As such, it clearly requires a different structure and atmosphere from the other communication functions. A typical structure is shown diagrammatically in Figure 14:1 and an example of suitable terms of reference and constitution are given in Appendix 7.

The consultative system is based upon the natural operating unit, say a production department in a manufacturing unit, or a sales force. It is the means by which operators, on the one hand, can influence their immediate environment and the manager, on the other, has a sounding board for his policies and practices. It relies upon an adequate information flow system related to the unit. The information should include measures of the unit's performance, contemplated changes, both short and long term, the discussion of objectives and their translation into action. The manager takes decisions in the light of the discussion and arranges the appropriate action. He can, for example, co-opt an inspector for a discussion on quality and subsequently require a report from him. When a matter arises which is outside the manager's discretion, he can either take it up through the normal chain of command or suggest that it is brought up for discussion at a higher level of the system—the works advisory council.

A typical departmental productivity panel consists of eight or nine members. They will include the departmental head and senior union representatives as *ex officio* members, a superintendent or foreman, and a representative from each section, or part of a section, where there are more than (say) thirty constituents. The main duties and responsibilities of the various panel members and of the constituents are outlined in Appendix 8. Perhaps it should again be emphasised that we do not advocate management by committee. On the other hand, it is likely that once a consultative system such as has been described is functioning properly—and the maturity of the discussion has to be experienced to be believed—much greater powers will be entrusted to it. Thus we have shown in Figure 14:1, that sub-committees of the works advisory council deal with the canteen, apprentice training, safety and a suggestions scheme. The latter deserves separate comment (see below).

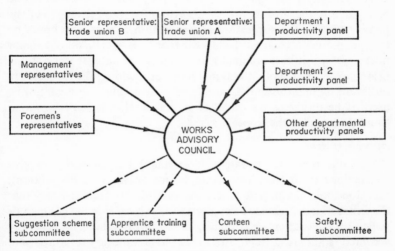

FIGURE 14:1 INTEGRATED JOINT CONSULTATIVE STRUCTURE

Role of the suggestion scheme

The history of suggestion schemes is not a very happy one. There are many reasons, but the more important are:

1   *Their purpose is incorrectly diagnosed.* The main purpose of a suggestions scheme is not to obtain brilliant ideas which will

radically increase productivity. The number of such ideas emanating from the shop floor is very limited indeed, and most ideas come from management. The main purpose is to encourage people to think about different ways of doing things; to get them to accept the idea of change. Thus all suggestions should be considered and discussed with the persons making them.

2   *It is usually too difficult to make a suggestion.* Many schemes require the suggestion to be set down in writing (in triplicate?) and accompanied by diagrams, drawings and full descriptions. This is far too difficult for the average man.

3   *Suggestions take too long to process.* This is especially so when the reward is related to estimates of the savings.

These problems can be overcome by a scheme such as that contained in Appendix 9.

The essentials are that (*a*) the only information required in the first place is the area in which improvement is suggested; (*b*) the person offering the suggestion is seen within twenty-four hours by two people competent to decide whether it is worth taking up or not; and (*c*) if it is, a nominal award is made at once. If it is not, the person receives a note thanking him for making the suggestion, outlining its main essentials and briefly indicating why it cannot be used. If he disagrees his outlet is, of course, that which is common to all grievances: the appeals system.

Appeals system

Where one man (for example, a foreman) has authority to give instructions to another (for example, an operator in his section), occasions sometimes arise where the subordinate feels strongly that the instruction which has been given to him is outside the company's policy on the matter, or is unfair, biased or prejudiced by generally accepted standards. Such situations arise in every organisation. Almost all these situations can be resolved by the subordinate and his supervisor together in a mature and objective manner, but it is only realistic to expect that from time to time there will arise occasions where both will find themselves in genuine disagreement. A code of practice should be drawn up so that all employees will know what to do when these situations arise, and be able to solve them with the least possible delay and with the least possible interference to production. An example is shown in Appendix 10.

It should be noted that where such an appeal concerns a matter which is the subject of an agreement between the unions and the employers' federation, the appeal must follow the agreed procedure for the settling of disputes which is set out separately. (See Appendix 11.)

Where an appeal arises and the foreman or chargehand cannot settle the matter himself, he should refer the matter to his own superior. That superior shall set a time for hearing the appeal at which he will call in both parties. The employee who is making the appeal (the appellant) may bring into the meeting, if he so desires, an advisor of his own choosing. After hearing both sides of the case, the superior will give his ruling.

If the appellant receives a ruling which he feels again is outside the company's policy or unfair he may appeal against that ruling to the next highest manager, and so on, until the managing director of the company is reached. His decision shall be final. Where successive appeals occur, it should be clear that each appeal is against a separate decision. Where a group of employees has a grievance in common against their common manager's decision, they may appoint a spokesman to conduct their appeal.

It will be obvious that the type of communications system outlined here has important implications for both management and trade unions. But these implications indicate only part of the rethinking that will be necessary if substantial progress is to be made.

If the personnel manager feels that an appeal is likely to cause immediate loss of production or severe damage to morale if it is not dealt with immediately, he may convene a meeting at which are present the appellant(s) and his (their) representative, the manager against whom the appeal is made, and all the intermediate managers in the direct executive chain. The personnel manager conducts the appeal.

Should an employee or group of employees refuse to accept a standard which applies to them, or an alteration to that standard, the following procedure should apply.

The disputed standard is discussed with the appropriate industrial engineer in the presence of the foreman. If agreement is not reached, the appropriate employee representatives—including one who has been trained in work study—discuss the standard with their superintendent and the industrial engineer. If agreement is still not reached, trial runs superintended by the chief industrial engineer or his deputy in the presence of the trained employee representative take place until agreement is reached. During the hearing of the appeal, work continues and the final decision should be applied retrospectively.

A recommended form of appeals procedure is outlined in Appendix 10.

Fifteen

Negotiation and Implementation

Companies which succeed in rationalising their system of wage payment establish—if their new structure is correctly devised and acceptable to employees—a new and improved framework of financial motivation, as well as a means of controlling their labour costs in the future. But the negotiation of a productivity agreement should produce more far-reaching benefits, important though these are.

The agreement should certainly remove employees' worst irritants and frustrations—clean up the "hygiene" factors, in terms of Herzberg's theory outlined in Chapter 2. In addition, it provides a unique opportunity for managements to re-structure the whole basis of their relations with employees, by changing the emphasis from containment and conflict to one of constructive involvement and co-operation. This claim is not idealistic, nor does it deny that conflicts of interest between management and employees will persist. It would be unhealthy if they did not. The claim does imply that conflict becomes a less frequent occurrence, and that the industrial relations policy and practice of the company cease to be centred on confrontation, grievances and disputes procedure. The disputes procedure (see Appendix 11) should no longer be the mainspring of the company's industrial relations policy—merely a necessary procedure to be called on occasionally, when problems of real magnitude or disputes with strong emotional overtones arise.

Of course, if dispute and grievance procedures do become a minor aspect of companies' industrial relations policy, it will only be as a result of major changes in the attitudes and relationships of the parties concerned. These changes will have been produced not by appeals from the managing director in the interests of company efficiency or export prospects, but by:

1   Re-structuring the roles and relationships of shop stewards and managers.

And, when this has been achieved, by:

2   Training managers and supervision through practical exposure to a new management style.

The basis on which these two requirements may be satisfied is a policy of involvement, participation, communication—or whatever abstract term means seeking to draw people's constructive abilities by behaving towards them as though they had a contribution to make and a contribution which was needed. Simply, it means a supportive rather than a coercive attitude to employees on the part of management.

Developing and negotiating a broad and comprehensive productivity agreement presents the company with a real opportunity to effect this change. It begins with the way the agreement is developed and negotiated.

Negotiation of agreement

Previous chapters have indicated how a comprehensive agreement can be developed by involving employees and their representatives. Specifically, attention should be drawn to two important and integral parts of any programme:

1   An attitude survey. Not the least of its benefits is the opportunity it gives management of demonstrating that it wishes to take account of employees' views in preparing for a programme of change.

2   Job evaluation by the direct consensus method, which involves shop stewards and employees' representatives in establishing a rank order of jobs and in drawing up proposals for a grade structure.

In addition we have examined the means of establishing a "share of prosperity" element as the third tier of a wages structure, one of the main functions of which is to provide an effective focus for obtaining the co-operation and involvement of employees in seeking greater efficiency and higher productivity. This, we have suggested, should be secured through a consultative communications structure based on departmental productivity panels.

Before such a third tier is established and productivity panels set up, the agreement will have to be negotiated and implemented. The way management sets about this is crucial if more constructive relations are to be established with employees.

Students of the productivity agreements which have been widely publicised will have noticed two different approaches to the way a comprehensive agreement is negotiated. On the one hand, an efficient management examines its company's problems of labour utilisation in detail, and presents the union with a comprehensive agreement designed to remove the more serious restrictions. This approach is typified by the Esso company's agreement at Fawley. On the other, some agreements have been developed by involving employees' representatives from the outset and asking them to come up with solutions to the problems of labour productivity. The agreement negotiated by the Shell Company at its Carrington works is a good example of this type of approach.

In our view, this latter is the more suitable basis for a productivity agreement which seeks to make fundamental changes to a company's industrial relations. The Fawley method separates management and employees—whose representatives, confronted with the results of management initiative, assume their habitual role of criticism and confrontation. But as we have sought to demonstrate, the development of an effective productivity agreement in a labour-intensive, operator-controlled manufacturing concern requires much more than identifying problems of restrictive practices or excessive overtime and inviting shop stewards to find solutions. Such an approach would be superficial, to say the least.

Shop stewards cannot, and should not, be asked to carry out an analysis in depth, like that set out in Part Two of this book. They should, however, be involved at the earliest possible stage in considering much of the information obtained from the analysis. Their involvement in establishing a grade structure has been outlined already. They should then be shown how their negotiations over the years have resulted in the generally inequitable earnings levels revealed by the wage and earnings analysis.

The stewards should be given the results of the attitude survey. This sometimes reveals differences between them and the people they represent. As a result, it encourages a more responsible attitude on the stewards' part towards the changes proposed.

The information obtained about the effectiveness of current incentive schemes should be presented and discussed, together with management's suggestions for revitalising or introducing better systems of bonus payment. The implications of such proposals, particularly if they involve a move from individual to large group incentives, need to be fully explored at a series of meetings. Management will have the opportunity of showing that it really wants shop stewards' opinions and wishes to involve them in developing the scheme.

In all these areas, we suggest, there is a greater degree of common interest than of conflict. The areas of conflict should be left until new relations and a degree of mutual trust have been built up. Where is disagreement likely? Which areas will become the subject of negotiation? Divergences of view are likely to centre on:

1   What employees will receive under the agreement—more specifically the levels of earnings which are proposed.
2   What employees will be asked to achieve for what they are to be offered; in other words, the productivity increase which the detailed analysis of the feasibility study has identified, and the ways in which the increase is to be obtained. The latter will include such considerations as higher operator performance, increased flexibility, job enlargement, and the accuracy and impact of productivity measures and incentive proposals.

There will be disagreement about some of the proposals, and both sides will have to compromise. But if the feasibility study has been carried out thoroughly, negotiations will be based on facts and not, as before, on subjective opinion. Accurate factual information disciplines negotiation, while a comprehensive agreement gives an opportunity for the formulation of fresh proposals which cut through the inhibitions of the existing situation.

Devising programme for negotiation and implementation

We have suggested already that employees and shop stewards should be informed and involved at the feasibility study stage. Once management has a sufficiently accurate assessment of costs and benefits for it to decide to go ahead, then discussions with shop stewards should start.

The programme for these meetings should take major aspects of the agreement in succession, and each meeting would consider the facts (obtained through the feasibility study) about the subject under consideration. Management may in some cases put up tentative proposals as a basis for discussion; in others, it will draw out the shop stewards' suggestions for improvement. The most important aspects are likely to be:

1   The rationalisation of the wage structure, and the implications.
2   The "variable" element, its measurement and implications.
3   The potential increase in productivity and its effects on such things as job security, overtime levels and job content.
4   The security-of-employment plan.

And, last only because it is the subject of most immediate concern to employees, the most likely conflict area; one which can only be discussed meaningfully when a measure of agreement has been reached on the other subjects:

5   The proposed level of earnings and the components of the wage structure.

While discussions with shop stewards need not necessarily follow this order, it has been found logical in most cases.

Certainly item 5 should wherever possible be left till last. Management should not enter into negotiations on earnings levels on the basis of a market-place haggle. Its offer should be as attractive as possible, and based on an accurate assessment of what the company can afford in the light of the identifiable benefits. When this is done the actual earnings levels are often acceptable to the unions, and discussion centres round their distribution—for example, differentials between grades, the relationship of direct and indirect employees' earnings, premium payments, redundancy terms and the protection of earnings allowances.

Management should be guided to a large extent in these areas by shop stewards' suggestions, monitoring their proposals by the results of the attitide survey as a check that stewards are reflecting employees' views. In this way conflict is reduced, and the stewards are channelled into more positive, constructive roles.

There are certain objectives which must be established when negotiating the agreement. The most important is the restoration of equity to the payment system if it has become anomalous. We have said that wage structures should be established across a factory or geographical site, so that a company pays approximately the same in all areas for similar work and performance. Investigation of a wage structure often reveals that the highest paid groups, whose earnings levels are the result of the slackest standards or the loosest rate fixing, have the highest potential increase in productivity. According to a strict interpretation of Government criteria, they are entitled to a full share of the benefits if they achieve this improvement. This would only produce even greater inequities in earnings levels within the factory or across the site. Management should therefore insist on a "pooling" of the productivity potential so that an equitable wage structure is established.

Where an agreement of this type is concluded for a factory employing several hundred or more employees working in a number of different divisions, departments or sections, it is most unlikely that it can be introduced overall at one time. The main reason for staggering the programme of implementation is likely to be the time needed to establish the performance standards by which productivity will be measured and employees' earnings determined. The time will vary according to the size of the site or factory, the staff resources the company can make available, and the type of measurement to be used. In the last case, for example, a full work measurement programme will take appreciably longer to implement than where financial ratios or statistical measures are to be the means of determining productivity and the employees' share of the benefits.

Thus the site or factory agreement will, in essence, set out a defined programme of implementation according to agreed principles, policies and financial returns. The practical implementation of the agreement will take place according to such a programme on the factory floor and will depend upon the relations and degree of understanding between managers, supervisors and employees. There is, therefore, a major communications and training need to be satisfied.

Communicating information about the agreement

We shall consider management's communication and information needs in Chapter 16; here we are concerned with these aspects as far as employees are concerned. The proposed changes cannot be imposed on employees, however desirable and beneficial they may appear. Employees must find them acceptable. The implications of this simple proposition are of great importance. Union representatives are unlikely to make any firm decision about the agreement on the employees' behalf: they will refer it to their members, so that the decision will be truly democratic. Virtually all employees will have their say through the votes they cast.

Although the employees may be guided by their representatives, they are not so easily swayed against what they feel is their better judgement. In one case a convenor of shop stewards, who was anxious for reasons of personal prestige to sign a productivity agreement, arranged a mass meeting of employees when the negotiations seemed near to success. Over-estimating the support for the agreement, he tried to "bulldoze" them into allowing him to conclude the agreement but the attempt backfired. The meeting broke up in confusion after a vote of "no confidence" in the convenor had been carried by acclamation. Two days later he was forced to resign and negotiations started again with his successor.

In most cases the power rests directly with the employees, and it is primarily they who must be convinced, not union officials. Putting it another way, there is little chance of success if union officials and shop stewards are antagonistic, but conversely it does not mean there are no major obstacles once union and shop steward support has been obtained.

As every employee will have a say in whether or not the agreement is signed, so each individual will decide on the basis of how he considers it affects him. This means that everyone must be given the facts about what implementation would mean to him personally. It is a truism that ignorance breeds fear and distrust. If people are not given specific information, they will fear the worst—often justifiably.

Communications with employees must therefore be programmed carefully along the following lines:

1   At the feasibility study stage, employees and their representatives should be told of the company's intention of investigating the practicability of a productivity deal. Their co-operation should be actively sought in specific areas such as job evaluation and the administration of an attitude survey. (It is worth remarking here that the writers have never been refused

permission to carry out an attitude survey by employees. Managements are another matter!)

2 Once the practicability of devising and implementing an agreement has been established, and discussions with shop stewards can usefully start, employees should be informed of the fact. The means of so doing should be discussed with the shop stewards. The stewards may take the responsibility on themselves, but management should ensure that employees *are* told and take steps to augment the union's channels of communication if they prove inadequate.

3 Progress reports on the meetings with the shop stewards should be issued and put up on notice boards. The stewards should be keeping their members informed on how discussions are proceeding, and this process should be augmented through line management's communication channels —primarily through supervisors. At this stage, feed-back is essential, and arrangements should be made to ensure that it is obtained. Supervisors have a crucial role to play here, since in many cases to rely exclusively on feed-back from shop stewards is leaving too much to chance.

4 When the agreement has been worked out in detail and the negotiators feel that as far as they are concerned agreement is virtually complete, the major communication exercise should be undertaken. This would comprise the following steps:

(a) A written communication should be given to each employee personally. This is probably most suitably devised as a pocket-sized booklet, attractively produced. (An example is shown in Appendix 12.)

(b) Line management and supervisors should be informed of the likely impact of the agreement as far as the people they are responsible for are concerned. A series of meetings should then be arranged at which supervisor and shop steward answer their group's question. When these general queries have been answered, the supervisor, with the shop steward, should see each employee individually and tell him how the agreement will affect him in respect of earnings, position in the revised grade structure and other aspects of employment. Any further questions are then answered. In this way the scope of the agreement and its individual impact are conveyed to each employee, and the employee can decide his attitude

170

on the basis of detailed, specific information. Employee acceptance of the proposals will be much more likely—provided always, of course, that the agreement does offer worthwhile and tangible benefits.

5   Finally, equally careful preparation and communication will be required when the time comes to implement the agreement in the department or section. The departmental productivity panel described in Chapter 14 will be one of the main vehicles of communication, and it should be set up before implementation starts. The panel's first task should be to help ensure that the agreement is put into practice with the minimum of friction and the maximum effect. This is a challenging task. It is essential that the right climate of relationships is established at the outset, and that meetings are not allowed to degenerate into a series of complaints, demands and accusations. The major responsibility here is management's; more specifically the departmental head, advised by the personnel function. It is, however, a depressing fact that, as presently constituted and manned, many personnel departments are unable to provide the expertise needed to advise management constructively. Yet it is in such areas that their true role is to be found.

This chapter has sought to give practical advice about the negotiation and communications aspects of implementing a productivity agreement. The framework it sets out will obviously require amendment in the light of each company's particular situation. However, the methodology, and the philosophy on which it is based, have, we believe, a more universal application. If a company's approach to implementing the changes follows the lines suggested here, a basis will have been established on which the company's industrial relations can be transformed. If, on the other hand, the agreement is implemented only after conflict, disagreement, industrial action and the use of sanctions by both sides, then the roles and attitudes of manager and shop steward, or supervisor and employee, will remain unchanged and the company's main requirement will be a good disputes procedure. It will probably be calling on it in the future.

Part V

AFTER THE AGREEMENT

16	*Implications for Management*	175
17	*Implications for Trade Unions*	183
18	*Conclusion: Movement towards Comprehensive Productivity Agreements*	191

Sixteen

Implications for Management

We are now at the stage when we can draw together the principal themes of this book and discuss the implications for management of negotiating and implementing a productivity bargain in depth. Within the term "management" it is important to include supervision, and so the effect upon the role of the foreman will also be examined.

An agreement may be devised and implemented with two separate and distinct objectives in view:

1   To bring order into the industrial relations situation and restore management's ability to exercise some control over the company's industrial relations and wage–work relations.
2   To create a new style of management and a creative work climate.

Most managements enter into productivity bargaining with the first object in mind (we ignore agreements which are devised merely to get round the Government's incomes policy). They are seeking to correct a disordered, uncontrolled industrial relations situation which is full of disincentives to higher productivity and hindrances to managerial action. Managements are increasingly aware of their responsibility for such situations, which have arisen largely because:

". . . in general, managements pay too little attention to the effects which their own practices have on work-place bargaining. Many fail to think out carefully which procedures are the most effective to secure order in the work-place, what the results of their payment systems are on the structure of bargaining within their establishments and, most common of all, what the role of different levels is in handling matters arising from the workshop floor." [Arthur Marsh, *Managers and Shop Stewards*, Institute of Personnel Management, 1963.]

The foreman has suffered particularly from this last situation. He is in day-to-day contact with the work-force and is responsible, nominally at least, for motivating them to an optimum standard of performance. He has first-hand experience of employees' frustrations, at the inequities which so frequently exist in pay, conditions, required performance standards, and so on. He is subject to the pressures which the lack of proper policies enables or encourages shop stewards and employees to exert. Too often he does not know the extent of his authority to take decisions or has found that such authority, defined for situations of thirty years ago, is inappropriate in a time of full employment. He sees shop stewards appealing over his head to the higher levels of management and often finds his superiors do not support him in disputes over the decisions he has taken. There is currently a good deal of discussion over the problems which beset the foreman today. Most of his problems stem from inadequate definition of his role in relation to the realities of the balance of power in industry, and from the inadequacy of companies' industrial relations policies.

A detailed productivity agreement will provide the basis for an improved industrial relations policy and improved managerial control. But the agreement should do more than remove the anomalies from payment systems, performance standards and so on. This is important but of secondary significance. To draw an analogy with Herzberg's motivation–hygiene concept, such an agreement puts the "hygiene" situation right but fails to establish a positive motivational policy. This is much the more constructive aspect of negotiating a far-reaching productivity agreement.

Many companies are, of course, unwilling to go this far. They are not prepared to change their overall management style. All they want is to introduce a degree of order into their industrial relations and obtain improved control through the creation of coherent policies. But the companies which are prepared to rethink their style of management, and move towards one which is employee-oriented, are making more of the opportunities which a comprehensive agreement offers them. As the benefits are greater, so of course are the demands made on the managers concerned.

A productivity agreement can be the starting point of a managerial policy designed to create a positive motivational framework for management and employees. The agreement is not therefore a once-for-all exercise, removing obstacles which have grown up over the years, but the beginning of a continuing policy of participative management. The foundations of this policy are:

1   Management's responsibility for taking the initiative in industrial relations.
2   The coincidence of many managerial and employee aims over large areas which can be established by involving employees in determining objectives and benefits where these are of direct concern to them.
3   The development of a problem-solving approach to areas of conflict between management and employees.

The implications for management of these policy foundations are considered in the following sections of this chapter.

Managerial initiative and industrial relations policy

Perhaps the most important long-term effect of the Labour Government's incomes policy since 1964 has been the pressure it has exerted on management to do something positive about pay and productivity matters. One hopes that this will prove to have lasting results and not disappear when the sanctions of the Prices and Incomes Act are removed.

If managements do retain the initiative, it will be because board-room thinking has been permanently affected. The signs are that such a realisation is occurring. No greater contribution to improved standards of management can be imagined than the boards of the major companies establishing as a fundamental policy the need to utilise their human resources to the optimum.

It is one thing to establish such a policy; quite another to implement it successfully. The implications of a readjustment on this scale are manifold, and the manner in which a company puts the policy into practice will itself reflect the extent of its understanding of the ways in which its human resources may be used most effectively. There are lessons to be learnt from the way companies which have developed positive employment and personnel policies have established and monitored them. In most cases, the personnel function

177

has had a key role, but the way it has performed its task has often led to difficulties.

Companies wishing to develop a constructive approach to the motivation of their employees have established a personnel department strong both in calibre and in numbers. Once such a department has been built up and had a chance to analyse the situation, it has prepared over a period of time, a series of policies on remuneration, conditions of service, management development, training and other employment conditions, for board approval. Once such approval is obtained, these policies have been imposed on management across the company.

The reception is often mixed. In so far as the policies remove anomalies in the existing situation and make the company more competitive in the appropriate labour market, they are generally welcomed by line management. Managers often accept, initially at least, the increasingly dominant role which the personnel department tends to play in negotiations with trade unions, since it releases them for what they often regard as more important activities.

However, managers have found in time that the policies are often restrictive and hinder them in carrying out their jobs. The personnel function seldom attempts to obtain management's commitment to its policies or to re-structure managerial attitudes towards the motivation of employees and the company's responsibilities towards them. Thus in the large and medium-sized company a gulf builds up between the professional personnel department and line management—particularly at the middle management level. Line managers are more and more irked at the restrictions which company-wide personnel policies impose on them, at the amount of time they take to administer, and at their irrelevance in some respects to what they believe are the real problems.

Personnel departments have often, by default, encouraged the growth of such views. They are often manned by well trained "professionals" who are knowledgeable about the range of techniques available for organising human resources. But these techniques—job evaluation, selection, training and induction procedures or joint consultative machinery—are too often introduced as ends in themselves: as justifications for the personnel function's existence rather than as a service that will help (and educate) managers to do their jobs more effectively.

When a company embarks on investigations into the feasibility of a detailed productivity agreement, it must deploy the necessary managerial resources to study the facts in depth. The personnel function should contribute to this effort but should not dominate it. Line management, management services and other functions should contribute members to a working party which is sufficiently objective to question all aspects of the existing situation and allow no sacred cows to go unchallenged—including existing personnel and industrial relations policies.

New management style

The need for a fully participative approach to the negotiation of a comprehensive productivity agreement has already been stressed. Such an approach is realistic in terms of the need to obtain employees' acceptance of radical change; it is also a more mature, more constructive approach to management and the motivation of employees. Line managers should be involved in the implementation of the plant-wide productivity agreement in each department. The introduction of the agreement into each department will provide a meaningful and important task for the first meetings of the departmental productivity committee, and each committee must be supported when major problems arise.

Senior managers and shop stewards should attend these early meetings from time to time and give the members guidance on the development of a constructive problem-solving approach. In some departments, conflict may have become entrenched, and a weekend away from the plant for management and employee representatives before their first meeting will help to break down barriers. This contact should give them a chance to discuss the fundamentals of their relationship, and can prove a most beneficial way of starting to restructure it. Managers and shop stewards have to undergo the experience of trying to establish a constructive relationship before they believe it is desirable and can produce results. Afterwards, neither side can understand why they used to be so antagonistic or why there were so many sources of conflict.

One danger to guard against is failure to obtain the full involvement of managers, supervisors and shop stewards, with the agreement being thrashed out by a small central negotiating committee and then imposed on managers and foremen by their bosses and on the employees by senior shop stewards. It is not sufficient to develop

179

a constructive, problem-solving climate in such a central committee if the negotiation and implementation of the agreement are to contribute to improved industrial relations at all levels. Individual managers, supervisors, shop stewards and employees must be involved, through a programme of carefully planned implementation. Real change is obtained, not by exhortation (as governments have found) but by restructuring the situation in which people find themselves and providing a means of establishing relations based on common interests.

Role of the foreman

Senior management initiates the changes required by the productivity deal, determines the objectives to be sought and plans the strategy for their attainment. Middle management should be involved in the detailed preparatory work of analysis, in the negotiations and in the first stages of implementation, so that it will feel the stimulus to change its relationships with employees through participation in the decisions which affect it. If management creates the opportunity and structures the change, the foreman is confronted with the challenge of making it work.

The day-by-day administration of the principal aspects of the agreement will be the concern of supervision. An effective agreement will have made the supervisor's job more rewarding, certainly in the short term and, it is to be hoped, in the long term also. The changes will require a positive response, and not all foremen will be able to meet the new demands. They are often conditioned to mere progress-chasing by incentive schemes which pass the control of wage–work relationships to employees, and to seeing their responsibility for planning the work load, motivating employees or determining quality dwindle away. These responsibilities must be restored to them and—guided by appropriate control systems and specialist services—shared, where appropriate, with employees. This policy recognises the need for supervision to manage, with the willing consent and co-operation of employees, and to build gradually, where technology allows, a motivational climate that will enrich the jobs of the production or service workers.

Some foremen look back nostalgically to the autocratic days when the bowler hat symbolised their authority. Nothing replaced this authority when it vanished in the post-war period. Only a defined and integrated policy which seeks to maximise the interests of employer and employed will provide an adequate replacement.

The foreman's role will change and he needs to be taught new skills and concepts. Both short- and long-term supervisory training needs can be identified when a productivity agreement is being implemented. In the short term, supervisors must be told about the changes proposed, and their impact on them clearly explained. They may not accept the changes; many will not. Those able to adapt will be identified soon enough—provided they are told in the first place, clearly and practically, the detailed changes the agreement seeks to introduce. The likely problems of increased productivity must be explained—for example, the bottlenecks which may occur as the production planning and control system is strained, or the resistance to new incentive schemes which employees will initially display. Foremen must understand the aims and mechanics of departmental productivity panels, particularly how they relate to their own jobs. Employees' rights under appeal or arbitration systems will need to be stressed, since the foreman will be the first to encounter employees' resistance to change.

A short-term training programme designed to provide supervisors with a comprehensive introduction to the impact of a productivity bargain is shown in Appendix 13.

In the longer term, as the foreman's role changes radically, a permanent long-term training programme based on detailed analysis of the new requirements of his job must be developed. The various training boards have laid down the procedure by which properly designed programmes are developed. They are founded on this detailed analysis of the job and the consequent training needs. The extent to which the foreman's role needs re-structuring should be established following the implementation of the agreement, and the training programme drawn up then.

Summary

The introduction of the type of productivity agreement described in this book will affect employees both at management level and on the shop floor. The greatest demands will fall on middle managers and foremen. Only if management at these levels accepts the proposed changes in management style, based on "joint regulation of the employment situation" with employee representatives, will a more positive industrial relations climate emerge. The personnel function has a most important part to play. It will have to change from "fire fighting" and "trouble shooting" to giving managers positive guidance in the implementation of the agreement, in ensuring that the communication channels—particularly at departmental level—operate constructively, and in devising appropriate training programmes.

The final result of this programme should be to ensure that line management assumes its responsibility for industrial relations and the motivation of employees. The climate management creates must recognise the power situation on the shop floor. Organised labour's considerable power is too often exercised without responsibility because management is unwilling to share it. We need more responsible trade unions, shop stewards and employees: it is in management's interest to help develop them.

Seventeen

Implications for Trade Unions

Productivity bargaining highlights many of the problems which face the trade unions. The effective influence they can exert through national agreements has been declining steadily over the years, as the relationship of nationally negotiated rates of pay to actual earnings levels has become increasingly obscure. The report of the Royal Commission on Trade Unions and Employers' Associations emphasised the increasingly important role of the shop steward and the relative decline in the influence of full time union officials, who work under heavy pressure, reacting to problems created by un-regulated workshop bargaining. In so far as productivity bargaining introduces order and equity into a factory's industrial relations, these pressures will be reduced. However, there is a possibility that the productivity agreement will have been developed by the manage-ment and shop stewards, leaving no meaningful role for the union official. There are already indications of these tendencies and they carry important implications for the future organisation of the trade unions.

Impact on national agreements

The unions have contributed to the retention of national negotiating procedures long after they have become irrelevant to their members' needs. Individual union leaders, such as Mr Les Cannon of the Electrical Trades Union, have taken a lead in condemning this reliance on national agreements, but only recently have unions begun to co-operate with employers in certain industries to amend this basic framework. Employees and unions in the chemical industry, for example, have signed a "Joint Agreement on the Principles and Procedures of Productivity Bargaining" which specifically encourages the development of factory agreements within the framework of industry-wide minimum rates of pay and certain conditions of employment. The rubber and printing industries have established similar agreements, and there are clear indications that in the engineering industry both the employers' federation and the major trade unions are thinking along the same lines.

This trend is encouraging, as it means that formal collective bargaining arrangements are coming closer to the realities of industrial relations. The impact on trade union strength and organisation is likely to be considerable. At national level, it suggests that union leaders will be less involved in dramatic clashes with employers, needing the eleventh-hour intervention of a cabinet minister to avert deadlock and a damaging yet pointless strike.

Union leaders and headquarters will occupy different roles under a system which specifically encourages the development of realistic factory agreements. Union leaders will be concerned with the national framework within which such agreements are negotiated; in other words, they will establish, with employers' representatives, the collective bargaining strategy for the industry. The union headquarters will provide local union officials and shop stewards with detailed information about the sort of agreements which have been negotiated in their particular industry, and will monitor those that are implemented. This trend is already evident and one may expect the continued growth of union research and information departments. The resulting increase in the flow of accurate information to union headquarters about what is actually happening in individual companies and factories will help the unions to develop a realistic approach towards establishing effective national frameworks.

If these trends do continue, shop stewards will receive more constructive assistance from their unions and the result may well be their closer integration with the union organisation. The shop steward will need such help, since he is likely to experience most directly the effects of a swing towards realistic plant bargaining.

Role of shop stewards

Whether or not the impact of plant productivity bargaining on shop stewards improves the general state of industrial relations depends

184

primarily on management. There is no doubt that the opportunity exists. In industries such as vehicle manufacture, printing, steel, metal working, chemicals and many others, the shop steward is the most influential member of the union hierarchy. The spate of unofficial disputes in the summer and autumn of 1968 revealed where the real power lay, as the number of man-hours lost through industrial action rose to its highest level for almost a decade. Union leaders might voice their opposition to the Government's incomes policy; the shop stewards and their members in a range of industries took action.

A number of important studies have analysed the increasing influence of the shop steward's role and its implications. [See particularly research paper number 1 of the Royal Commission on Trade Unions and Employers' Associations, *The role of shop stewards in industrial relations* and research paper number 10, *Shop stewards and workshop relations*, HMSO, 1966.] These studies reveal the growth of work-place bargaining and the lack of formal agreements or procedures on which to base this bargaining. They suggest that while the influence of shop stewards was bound to grow in a full-employment society, two factors have contributed particularly: the increasing irrelevance of national agreements to shop-floor realities, and management inertia in framing industrial relations policies. The trade unions themselves have failed to make adequate provision for shop stewards. Many union rule books fail to mention them; those that do are less than specific about stewards' responsibilities and powers. This is hardly surprising in view of the enormous variation, within and across industries, in what the shop steward does and achieves.

The general picture has been clearly set out in the report of the Royal Commission on Trade Unions and Employers' Associations. The image of the shop steward it reveals is completely different from the stereotype of the popular press. A national research officer of the General and Municipal Workers' Union, Mr Giles Radice, went so far as to describe the shop steward as "the hero of the Royal Commission report." [Address to the seventh session of the 38th summer conference of the Industrial Co-partnership Association, 1968.] To many people's surprise, perhaps, the Commission demonstrated the mutual respect between managers and shop stewards: "Four managers out of five thought shop stewards were either very efficient or fairly efficient." Ninety-five per cent of managers in the surveys conducted on behalf of the Commission thought that stewards were either very reasonable or fairly reasonable. Shop stewards reciprocated these views: "Almost all of them thought that management was either 'very reasonable' or 'fairly reasonable' in dealings with them." [Report of the Royal Commission on Trade Unions and Employers' Associations, Chapter 3, paragraph 124.]

The writers' experience does not entirely confirm this mutual admiration. Our own attitude surveys and interviews have revealed more suspicion and distrust than the above suggests. Nevertheless, on balance we would support the view that there exists a sound basic relationship between shop stewards and managers on which more constructive relations could be based.

A first step would be to regularise the position of the shop steward on "matters such as: facilities for holding elections; numbers and constituencies; recognition of credentials; facilities for consulting and reporting back to their members; facilities for meeting other stewards; the responsibilities of the chief shop steward (if any); pay while functioning as a steward in working hours; day release with pay for training. [Report of the Royal Commission on Trade Unions and Employers' Associations, Chapter 4, paragraph 182.] If such proposals are made, they will show the stewards that management explicitly recognises that they have an important role to perform. A change to a more constructive relationship may thus be carried through.

A comprehensive productivity agreement will recognise the shop steward's power. It will seek to involve him in the responsibility for establishing a rational industrial relations framework. It will make the shop steward's job more demanding, even if the frustrations are removed or at least reduced. Some stewards will be reluctant to accept with management joint responsibility for industrial and employee relations (so, of course, will many managers!). Most stewards react to the pressures of their members; it is only the minority who guide and foster employees' aspirations and requirements. Democratic leadership is no easy art.

This, however, is the role cast for the shop steward in productivity bargaining in depth, and it should be a continuing role. The steward will be asked to give a more specific lead to those whom he represents. There are dangers here, of course. The steward who becomes too enthusiastic about the proposals he is developing with management may come to be regarded as a "management man."

This is a possibility of which both stewards and management must be aware. A steward's power rests ultimately on the confidence his members have in him; if he becomes divorced from them, the progress made and the improved relations developed with management will be of no real value.

Two tangible and practical steps can be taken to help the shop steward adapt to his new role and assist employees' understanding of it. First, companies can provide the stewards with reasonable opportunities for talking to their members, both individually and in groups. Such facilities should be within the premises and, wherever appropriate, in works hours. (In this connection one wonders how many man-hours are lost by the insistence that union meetings should be held outside company premises. One shop steward described the results of such a policy: "If the weather is fine, I find it difficult to get the men back. Before the meeting's over, half of them will have drifted off home anyway. Mind you, if it's raining they're only too glad to get back inside and the meeting is always short.") When shop stewards are successfully involved in developing productivity agreements and monitoring their progress, good facilities for communicating with their members are not only essential but very much in the company's interests. The right to arrange meetings will not be abused if a good relationship has been built up between management and shop stewards.

The second step which can be taken to strengthen the shop steward's position is the provision of training. In the last analysis, the best training stewards can have is participating with management in decision-making processes. But they can be helped to take this responsibility. Here again, management initiative is called for in setting up a training programme. This is not to say that management should run the programme. Many unions are unwilling for their stewards to be subjected to "brainwashing." Universities, technical colleges and the Workers' Educational Association are often asked to run shop steward training courses to surmount this objection. This practice establishes the degree of impartiality which the unions feel is necessary.

There are problems with this approach, however. Such courses tend to be theoretical and general in nature, covering such subjects as "the economics of the business," "British industrial relations," and "the structure of the trade unions." Academic lectures of this type make little impact on the average shop steward. Theory and generality need to be related directly to his experience and his problems. External agencies are unable to do this; they lack the time to probe a company's situation in detail and build up case study material from such an analysis.

If, therefore, the programme is to be based on company realities, management and shop stewards (with the help of the appropriate union officials) should agree the content of the course jointly. Management can provide the facilities and whatever managerial participation is called for. The unions, and perhaps the Trades Union Congress, will similarly make a major contribution. An imaginatively designed programme should use participative techniques and case study material from the company. In so doing it may provide the starting point for the joint consideration of solutions to existing problems. It should examine the basic economics of running a business by reference to the company's cost structure and profitability; it should also consider some of the principles on which industrial relations and personnel policies are, or should be, based. In this way, interest will be maintained and the course may achieve its objective: a better informed and more knowledgeable group of shop stewards.

It is sometimes said that managements get the shop stewards they deserve—a statement hotly disputed by companies with militant stewards. Evidence suggests that there is as much truth in this as in any generalisation which is based on a broad view over a large and rather intangible area. If it is so, managements have an opportunity they ought to take. Where companies do regularise the role of their stewards and establish more constructive relations at plant level, permanent union officials will also feel the effect.

Role of union officials

The Donovan report revealed widespread shortages in the numbers of full-time trade union officials in some major unions. The most seriously affected appeared to be the Amalgamated Engineering Union, which in 1966 had a ratio of 6807 members to each full-time union officer. The report suggested that the growth of productivity bargaining at factory level will necessitate closer relations between officials and their shop stewards on account of the demands such agreements make. The Royal Commission's research paper number 4 on productivity bargaining concluded as a result that "it will be

essential for trade unions to increase the numbers of their officials."
[Page 29, paragraph 132.]

The writers have assisted in the negotiation of many productivity
agreements and, in most of them, negotiations were carried out with
the shop stewards alone. The full-time official was always informed
but, doubtless because of pressure of work, was generally willing to
let the shop stewards undertake the negotiations without his assistance. This contributed to the rate of progress and the frequency of
meetings: no delays were caused by a full time official's crowded
diary. When he did become involved, it was usually because the
negotiations had run into difficulty, and he then fulfilled his normal
role of resolving crises.

This experience indicates that in some industries the full time
official may be unable to participate in large-scale productivity
bargaining owing to pressure of work. If the shop stewards then
reach agreement without him, the union official's influence may
eventually disappear as far as the employees of that particular company
are concerned. As a result, the union's strength in the company will
depend even more on the shop stewards rather than on its paid
officials.

When union officials cannot take part in negotiations they might
well consider how they can keep themselves informed of develop-
ments so that they can advise and guide shop stewards during
negotiation. They can bring a useful measure of objectivity to the
situation and thus ensure that the agreement does not contain
provisions which might have awkward implications for their members in other companies in the district.

This possibility of external influence in the course of negotiations
is greatest when they involve the Amalgamated Engineering Union.
The district officials of this union are often closely controlled by
district committees which tend to exert a negative influence whenever
comprehensive and far-reaching agreements affecting AEU members
are referred to them. The vetting powers which these committees can
exercise over negotiations affecting AEU membership in the district
are irrelevant to the needs of plant productivity bargaining, but can
provide a formidable obstacle to progress. Consideration of an
agreement by a district committee should be avoided where possible,
and this may mean a company setting out to negotiate with its shop
stewards only.

The role of the full-time official will therefore be affected by the

189

growth of plant productivity bargaining. In cases where successful agreements are negotiated without his involvement, his influence may diminish. When he is able to take a major role in negotiation, the converse will be true. But for all officials, the introduction of more coherence into companies' industrial relations will reduce the number of disputes—though when they do occur they are likely to be serious and to affect more people.

Finally, and most important, the local official will often be concerned with the negotiation of further factory-wide agreements on a regular basis after the first productivity agreement has been implemented. These may be negotiated irregularly or at specific renewal dates; they will cover all employees (provided companies set out to preserve a coherent wages structure) and may, where no third tier (or share-of-prosperity element) has been established, mean long and protracted negotiation. In the future, therefore, one may foresee fewer negotiations at plant level, with those that do occur being much more comprehensive and taking longer to reach agreement. Management and union officials must accept this as the price of maintaining an equitable structure for pay and conditions at plant level.

Eighteen

Conclusion: Movement Towards Comprehensive Productivity Agreements

In a book of this size, we have of necessity had to present separate aspects of the development and implementation of comprehensive productivity agreements. While it is necessary to separate the various aspects, we would emphasise that they form the elements of a closely integrated system of industrial relations. For example, while the three-tier wage structure is designed to provide a framework for establishing a remuneration policy appropriate to the needs of differing industries, it also provides the focus for a properly devised communications structure founded on departmental productivity panels. Similarly, the attainment of productivity increases by properly designed bonus systems, increased flexibility and job enlargement will only be meaningful if it is related to a security-of-employment plan which satisfies employees' need for job security. Consultants are sometimes accused of being technique-centred. In this book we have tried to show that techniques can only be regarded as useful tools which will assist in the solution of problems. The identification of the size and shape of the problem, and the framing of a comprehensive, long-term solution, lie at the heart of most companies' industrial relations situation.

It is the writers' belief that the time is ripe for a radical change. The negotiation of a detailed, comprehensive productivity agreement provides the vehicle for such a change, since it deals with many of the major issues in which management and employees have a common interest. While many issues are concerned, on one level, with familiar factors—earnings, security, productivity and so on—underlying them are pressures from employees for a more meaningful working environment and for more satisfying jobs. Employees are also seeking a more direct say in the aspects of employment which directly affect them. Industry will have to come to terms with this situation. Whether it does so through agreements of the type described here is a choice which companies themselves must determine.

Government policy since about 1964 has done much to create a climate favourable to change. After years of exhortation about the need for increased productivity and for control of incomes, the Prices and Incomes Act brought sanctions to bear. The "teeth" of the policy have proved to be somewhat less than razor-sharp, and the measurable results of the "freeze" and period of restraint very small. The rate of increase in earnings in the period before July 1966 was temporarily halted, but seems to have resumed at a similar pace.

But if the impact has been limited in terms of the control of increases in wages and salaries, it has been considerable from a psychological viewpoint. Managers, union leaders, shop stewards and employees have been made aware of the need for increased productivity and of the inequitable, inadequate results which traditional wage–work bargaining has produced.

Government agencies such as the Prices and Incomes Board have examined the main aspects of these problems in detail, and their ideas have found a wider and more receptive audience than hitherto. This despite the fact that their criteria for permitting wage increases above the norm have frequently proved unworkable. For example, they make no provision for the company which already uses its manpower efficiently. They fail to take account of the requirements of a vast range of service undertakings (notably the retail trade), for whom realistic productivity measurement is impracticable. For a limited period, however, and despite these inequities, the criteria set out the basic factors to which manufacturing companies (in particular) should turn their attention.

A growing number of companies are now grappling with these problems through the medium of factory productivity agreements. If factory agreements are negotiated on a wide scale, the effect on industry and industrial relations will be far-reaching. The Royal

Commission on Trade Unions and Employers' Associations put the position in a nutshell:

"The central defect in British industrial relations is the disorder in factory and workshop relations and pay structures . . . in most industries such matters cannot be dealt with effectively by means of industry-wide agreements. Factory-wide agreements can, however, provide the remedy."

But the Commission makes one all-important proviso about such agreements:

"All that is claimed for a factory agreement is that it is a means for the effective regulation of industrial relations within the factory where managers and workers choose to use it for that purpose."

For those who make such a choice we have tried to set out what is involved, the problems that will be met and the means of solving them so that the long term needs of the company and its employees are met. The prosperity of both depends on the degree to which such a reconciliation takes place and a constructive relationship between management and work-force is established.

—————————————Part VI—————————————

Appendices

1	*Impediments to Production*	197
2	*Multiple Regression Analysis*	200
3	*Attitude Survey*	204
4	*Criteria for a Successful Payment-by-Results Scheme*	210
5	*Assessment Form for a Graded Hourly Rate System*	212
6	*Employment Security Plan*	214
7	*Recommended Constitution for a Works Productivity Council*	222
8	*Notes for the Guidance of Committee Chairmen, Representatives and Electors*	228
9	*Recommended Constitution for a Suggestion Scheme*	231
10	*Recommended Appeals Procedure*	235
11	*Recommended Procedure for Settling Disputes*	238
12	*Proposals for a Productivity Agreement*	240
13	*Productivity Agreement and New System of Wage Payment*	242
14	*Supervisory—Appreciation and Training Programme*	252

Impediments to Production

This list of hindrances to production due to the organisation of work (restrictive practices) illustrates the most commonly encountered impediments. The list is intended to be handed to managers and supervisors so that they can indicate, in the columns on the right, the degree of importance of each item to their own company.

DESCRIPTION OF PRACTICE	SIGNIFICANCE TO COMPANY		
	High	*Tolerable*	*Low*
1 Timekeeping: late starting and early finishing.			
2 Carry-over of time booking.			
3 Unofficial stoppages for meeting purposes and meetings extended.			
4 Extension of official tea breaks.			
5 Stewards leaving shop without permission of foreman.			
6 Unions restrictions resulting in lower labour intake than would otherwise be possible.			
7 Shop stewards required to approve overtime.			
8 Claim by employees that "one in, all in" on overtime.			

197

9 Reluctance to accept double and treble shift working.

10 Resistance to changes in production methods that can reduce operational times.

11 Resistance to changes to grade of labour for job, e.g., skilled to semi-skilled.

12 Some unions demanding exclusive right to certain work in opposition to other unions.

13 Resistance to transfer of labour from one type of machine to another which may have been necessitated by absenteeism.

14 Objection by electricians to relatively simple connections being made by fitters, etc.

15 Absenteeism after weekend working.

16 Refusal to accept stop-watch in all departments.

17 Interchange of labour between departments where there are related trades.

18 Demand that certain jobs are the prerogative of certain shops in spite of inconvenience and change in technology.

19 Refusal by certain shops to allow recruitment when they have a wage claim in.

20 Refusal of employees to work with outside employees who are not union members.

21 Refusal to co-operate with outside contractors unless they are in appropriate unions.

22 Refusal to modify jigs and equipment
    that have been manufactured outside.

23 Limitation on recruitment of
    apprentices.

Please add any point not covered to which you desire to draw special attention.

DESCRIPTION OF PRACTICE	SIGNIFICANCE TO COMPANY		
	High	*Tolerable*	*Low*

Multiple Regression Analysis

Theory

Multiple regression analysis is a well established mathematical technique. Its use in the measurement of productivity and related factors is less well known. (See Chapter 4.)

Theory

The relationship between two directly proportional variables can be expressed by a straight line on a graph. It is possible to use this line to predict the value of one variable when the other is known. The relationship can be expressed mathematically in the form:

$$y = ax_1 + b$$

where a and b are constants.

The graphical form will normally be built up by measuring corresponding values of x_1 and y, which are then plotted as points on a graph. Should the points not fall accurately on a straight line, it will be necessary to draw the "best line" through the points. This "line of best fit" or "line of regression" is drawn so that the sum of the squares of the distances of all points from the line is minimal.

The scatter of points about the line of regression will only be small if all other related factors remain constant. If, however, a further factor x_2 varies in a manner which is directly proportional to y, it will be possible to create a three-dimensional model in which the relationship between all three variables is expressed by a straight line. The scatter of points about this new line should be less than would be possible in a two-dimensional representation. Since some scatter is likely to exist, the line of regression must be calculated as before. This line can be represented by the equation:

$$y = c_1x_1 + c_2x_2 + d$$

where c_1, c_2 and d are constants.

If another factor varies, then the scatter on our three-dimensional model will increase and we must turn to a four-dimensional representation. This must obviously be mathematical and of the form:

$$y = e_1x_1 + e_2x_2 + e_3x_3 + f$$

where e_1, e_2, e_3 and f are constants. This is essentially the best line through the points in four dimensional space.

It is possible in this way to build up a mathematical expression explaining the behaviour of y in terms of any number of variables which may affect it. Any point in time, substitution of the values for all the variables into the equation will give the value of y. The limitations on the number of variables which can be used in practice are considered later.

Procedure

The first step is to decide on the form of the relationship in general terms:

$$y = e_1x_1 + e_2x_2 + e_3x_3 + f$$

where y is the factor desired, x_1, x_2 and x_3 are variables on which y depends, and e_1, e_2, e_3 and f are unknown constants. Sets of values for all the y and x variables must be obtained and substituted in the above equation to give a series of equations of the form:

$$1.5 = 2.0e_1 + 3.5e_2 + 4.6e_3 + f$$
$$2.0 = 1.7e_1 + 3.8e_2 + 4.0e_3 + f \text{ and so on.}$$

The solution of these equations to give the values of e_1 e_2, e_3 and f which can be substituted in our original equation is called *multiple regression analysis*.

With normal simultaneous equations, a single discrete result is obtained when the number of equations is equal to the number of variables. With multiple regression analysis, the result is only the best approximation obtainable and hence it can be improved in accuracy by taking more equations. The final equation will be of the form:

$$y = 2.5x_1 + 3.4x_2 + 6.7x_3 + 4.0$$

In the future, any measure of corresponding values of x_1, x_2, x_3 will permit the calculation of the equivalent value of y.

Sources of data

It has been shown that corresponding values of *all* the variables must be available in order to set up the multiple regression analysis. Thus the factor desired, be it productivity or any other measure, must be defined and measurable by direct means. The required information can come from two sources:

1. Historical records may provide values for the factors involved. If we require a measure of productivity, the equation can be set up in terms of loose values or even hours worked—as long as there is reason to believe, in the latter case, that operator performance has been reasonably constant. After creation of the regression equation, activity sampling and production studies are necessary to establish true performance for comparison with those indicated by the existing system so that the equation can be recalibrated. Sampling work need only cover a sample of the work performed so that the recalibration can be quite rapid.

2. If no historical records are available for any or all of the major factors, it will be necessary to derive *all* values by activity sampling and production studies. This will inevitably be a long process, since observations must be made over the complete range of all variables. Unlike the setting of standard times, it is not necessary to cover as many permutations of the conditions.

Number of variables

The accuracy of the regression equation in explaining the behaviour of our main variable increases as more factors are used. However, this is only true if the number of values for each factor is increased proportionally. When no historical records are available, a good case will exist for the restriction to three or four factors.

Type of variable

The relationship between the various factors and the main variable must be linear if our regression equation is to give adequate representation over a reasonable range. In order to obtain a linear relationship, it may be necessary to use the powers of some variables and the products of others. The need for these special forms must arise from a logical assessment of the relation between variables and from the results of early trials.

Calculation

It is possible, though laborious, to calculate multiple regression by hand for up to four factors. It would be usual to use a computer for this work and programmes for this purpose are generally available.

Validity

The validity of the equation produced from the original information is checked against the data fed into it. The equation will not necessarily be valid for values outside the range of those originally considered. New sets of values should be collected by activity sampling to test the results.

Major method changes will invalidate the original results, and revision of the system will be required approximately every two years. Continuous monitoring of the variables as changes occur will provide adequate historical background when revision is required. The introduction of major new plant should be followed by an immediate reappraisal of the system.

Areas of application

Multiple regression analysis is particularly suitable for establishing productivity measures for groups of workers. Non-routine work involving a wide variety of products can more easily be handled in this way than by time study. Operations at the start and end of a production line are most easily considered, since the maximum amount of recorded information is usually available at these stages. Clearly defined groups of operators are preferable, since difficulties can arise where indirect workers are shared between groups.

This technique, used with care and insight, has a very wide application outside as well as within the manufacturing industry.

Attitude Survey

An example of a comprehensive attitude survey designed to determine employees' views on the company and possible areas of change. This survey was carried out by Associated Industrial Consultants Limited for the purposes of sociological analysis as outlined in Chapter 6.

As part of our investigation on pay and productivity we are carrying out a survey to find out employees' ideas and opinions about various things in your division and in the company.

We would like you to answer the questions honestly and frankly and give us your opinions freely.

Anything you tell us will be treated in the strictest confidence. No other employee of the company, including managers, will ever see your answers.

1   Site:
2   Division:
3   Present job:
   (*a*) Skilled.
   (*b*) Semi-skilled.
   (*c*) Unskilled.
4   Shift:
   (*a*) Days.
   (*b*) Nights.
   (*c*) Rotating day/night.
   (*d*) Other.

5   System of payment:
- (a) Flat time-work.
- (b) Payment by results.
- (c) Other.

6   Length of service:
- (a) Less than 1 year.
- (b) 1 year and under 5 years.
- (c) 5 and under 10 years.
- (d) 10 and under 15 years.
- (e) 15 and under 20 years.
- (f) 20 years or over.

7   Shop steward:
- (a) Steward.
- (b) Non-steward.

8   Male/female.

Written below is a list of statements that people might make about your division. After each one we would like you to say whether you "agree" or "disagree." There are no right or wrong answers; it depends on how you feel.

9   Management is fair in the way it treats employees.

10   You can rely on your foreman to get something done quickly when problems come up.

11   The managers are in close touch with what happens in their departments.

12   This company is a good company to work for if you want a secure job.

13   Under the present method of paying wages, some employees don't really deserve the money they get.

14   Employees' opinions are hardly ever considered by the management.

15   Trade union communications are readily available to me.

16   Foremen should take a firmer line on discipline.

17   It is preferable to work alone rather than in a group.

18   The unions are doing a good job for employees here.

19   You would be willing to work on shifts if it were necessary.

20   Managers here are in control of the situation.

21   Unions should have a much greater say in the running of the place.

Here are some more general questions about the company:

22 What is your overall opinion of this company as a company to work for?
  (*a*) Very good.
  (*b*) Good.
  (*c*) About average.
  (*d*) Poor.
  (*e*) Very poor.
23 What do you feel are the good features about working here?
24 And what are the poorer features?
25 What, in your opinion, are the main changes that have taken place over the last few years?

In your opinion, how much importance does your division seem to place on each of the following things?

GREAT/SOME/VERY LITTLE
26 Safety:
27 Quality of work:
28 Working conditions:
29 Training:
30 High output:
31 Fair wages:
32 Keeping people informed:
33 Job security:
34 One hears a lot about productivity these days. In your own words, can you tell us three ways in which employees here could help to improve productivity in the company?

People have different ideas on the best way of improving productivity. Please indicate whether you think the methods listed below will lead to improved productivity in your division or not.

YES/NO/DON'T KNOW
35 Improving quality:
36 Reducing waste of materials:
37 Increasing the pay of all employees:
38 Training employees to do a number of different jobs:

39 Introducing more shift work:
40 Taking on more employees:
41 Using better methods of
  working:
42 Having greater discipline on
  absenteeism and lateness:
43 Raising operator
  performance:

Now we'd like to know about wages and the system of wage payment:

44 What is your weekly pay on average before tax and deductions (approximately)?
45 All in all, what do you think of your pay for the work you do?
  (*a*) Very good.
  (*b*) Quite good.
  (*c*) Reasonable.
  (*d*) Rather poor.
  (*e*) Very poor indeed.

Here is another series of questions with "agree/disagree" answers.

46 An incentive bonus scheme is the only way to keep production up.
47 The company needs far fewer different basic rates of pay.
48 Jobs requiring greater skill should have higher pay.
49 As far as bonus pay is concerned, it's not worth working harder.
50 Rates of pay in one group or section should not be tied to the rates in other sections.
51 You don't need to work overtime to get a reasonable living wage.
52 Wages here are better than at most other companies in the district.
53 Employees in some divisions deserve to earn more than employees in other divisions.
54 The company's present system of wage payment needs to be changed.

If the answer to 54 is "agree":

55 What changes would you like to see and why?

56 Do you feel that targets for jobs are necessary to help make sure the company is running efficiently?
   (a) Definitely necessary.
   (b) Probably necessary.
   (c) Not really necessary.
   (d) Definitely not necessary.

57 Please complete this sentence in your own words:
   "The trouble with working in a big company like this is that

   . . . ."

58 Read the following list and indicate the *two* things which, to you personally, are of greatest importance in your work. Also pick the two which are of *least* importance to you:
   (a) Having friendly workmates.
   (b) Knowing what's going on in the division.
   (c) Being in a sick pay scheme.
   (d) Having a secure job.
   (e) Working close to home.
   (f) Getting high wages.
   (g) Having a job where one is not pushed for a high output.
   (h) Being on good terms with managers.
   (i) Having prospects for moving up to better jobs.
   (j) Making full use of one's abilities.
   (k) Having steady earnings.
   (l) Being in a pension scheme.

59 How well do you feel your division is doing at the present time?
   (a) Extremely well.
   (b) Well.
   (c) Holding its own.
   (d) Slipping a bit.
   (e) In a bad way.

60 And what about the company as a whole? Would you say it was doing:
   (a) Extremely well.
   (b) Well.
   (c) Holding its own.

(*d*) Slipping a bit.

(*e*) In a bad way.

61   In your opinion, what are the main problems currently facing the company?

62   What, in your view, are the things that seem to be worrying employees most?

63   Are there any other things you would like to mention?

Criteria of the Prices and Incomes Board for a Successful Payment-by-Results Scheme

This set of criteria by which the success of a payment-by-results system may be judged is extracted from Chapter 10, paragraph 255 of report number 65, *Payment-by-results systems*, published by the National Board for Prices and Incomes in May 1968. According to the board, a PBR system is working successfully when:

1   The rate of increase of average hourly earnings (excluding overtime and increases paid under industry-wide agreements or their equivalent in non-federated firms, and excluding also increases demonstrably attributable to increased worker effort) is $1\frac{1}{2}$ per cent or less a year.

2   The proportion of average earnings (excluding overtime) which takes the form of variable output bonus does not exceed one quarter.

3   Standards of performance are set by work measurement carried out by adequately trained staff whose consistency in rating is regularly checked.

4   Enterprise or industry agreements establish clear ground rules separating the process of pay negotiation from the setting of work standards and ensuring uniformity of practice in respect of the latter.

5   The "learning curve," or "improvement effect," is taken into

210

account when establishing work standards for new jobs and new workers, or revising them for old jobs.

6   The differentials between the pay of different occupational groups are determined in detail by job evaluation, or a systematic and comprehensive agreement (or both), and are specified, not merely in terms of basic rates, but of "standard earnings" or the equivalent.

7   The suitability and administration of the system has undergone a major investigation within the past three years.

Assessment Form for a Graded Hourly Rate System

Employee grading award scheme: skilled trades

The following example of an assessment form for use with a graded hourly rate system of payment, was used by Associated Industrial Consultants Limited, in connection with the installation of such a system at a large engineering group to determine increments to skilled craftsmen against three criteria, skill, rate of work and quality of work. The assessment is carried out by the foreman and approved by his immediate manager. (See Chapter 8.)

Name................ Clock number...... Department.......

		POINTS AWARD
1	*Range of skill* (interpolation allowed in five-point steps).	
	(*a*) Exceptionally versatile. Able to carry out a range of intricate and complex work in his department.	40
	(*b*) Experienced worker who is able to complete satisfactorily a wide range of work in his department, but is limited in some aspects of the more advanced type of job.	30
	(*c*) Can carry out all routine and straightforward tasks in his department without supervision.	20
	(*d*) Can complete only the simpler tasks in his department without help from supervision.	10

2   *Rate of accurate working* (BS 3138 (1959)).

(*a*) Very fast: equivalent to performance index of
     over 115.   45
(*b*) Above standard: equivalent to performance
     index of 105–115.   35
(*c*) Standard: equivalent to performance index of
     95–105.   25
(*d*) Below standard: equivalent to performance
     index of 85–95.   15
(*e*) Below standard: equivalent to performance
     index of 75–85.   5

3   *Quality of work* (interpolation allowed in five-
       point steps).

(*a*) Works to the highest standards of craftsman-
     ship, reliability and safety in all aspects of his
     work.   25
(*b*) Works reliably and to good standards of
     craftsmanship and safety on all but the most
     complex work without supervision.   20
(*c*) Observes reasonable standards of craftsman-
     ship and safety and is reliable on straight-
     forward work. Requires careful checking on
     more advanced type of work.   10
(*d*) Observes satisfactory standards of craftsman-
     ship, reliability and safety on the simpler
     work of the department.   5

Previous points..................... Total points..........

Signed.................. Approved.............. Date......

Employment Security Plan

In Chapter 13, the importance of preparing a detailed security of employment plan was emphasised. The following model, which was prepared for a large multi-site engineering company, sets out means by which a company should try to avoid redundancy, criteria for deciding which employees will be made redundant if it is unavoidable, periods of warning and notice, compensation and appeals procedure. It is fully consistent with the Contracts of Employment and Redundancy Payments Act.

Introduction

The sole aim and objective of this plan is to provide *all* employees with the maximum possible security of employment. The company recognises that security of employment is one of the primary needs of working life. Consequently it will, as in the past, take all reasonable steps to prevent the occurrence of redundancy. Nevertheless, in a period of increasingly rapid technological and economic change, the possibility of redundancy cannot be ruled out. Through careful and continuous manpower planning, however, the company will endeavour to ensure that redundancy is a last resort, so that it takes place only when all possible measures to prevent it have been fully explored.

Measures to avoid redundancy

Attrition

1   Whenever the company reaches a position where it is anticipated that manpower will be surplus to requirements, recruit-

214

ment of *those employees possessing the particular skill or skills which are potentially affected* shall be curtailed or halted. Recruitment will first be halted or curtailed in the department where redundancy threatens. Only if this is seen to be insufficient to deal with the problem shall recruitment be halted or curtailed on a factory-wide basis.

2   Where redundancy threatens staff employees, recruitment may be halted or curtailed at both factories.

3   It must be realised that although the company will consult with employee representatives on the locations at which recruitment is to be halted or curtailed, the ultimate decision in this respect rests with the company.

4   Similarly, whilst halting recruitment altogether may seem the most expedient measure by which a work-force can be reduced, the company must take such measures as it considers necessary to maintain a balanced age structure of the labour force. For this reason the company reserves the right to halt or curtail recruitment as the particular circumstances of any given case may demand.

Transfer

1   Where recruitment has been halted or curtailed in one or both factories, all employees shall have the right to transfer to any vacancies which exist within the same factory. In addition, staff employees may transfer to any vacancies which exist in the other factory.

2   Where vacancies exist in a limited number within the same factory, transferring employees shall be selected on the basis of seniority within the factory, all other things being equal.

3   Where transfer for staff is to the other factory, selection will be made by calling for volunteers.

4   All transferring employees will be retrained, where this is necessary, and those transferred to a lower-graded occupation will continue to receive their basic wage or salary for the old grade for a period of twelve weeks, or until earnings are equal to the average in the original occupation, whichever is the shorter period.

5   Where any employee unreasonably refuses suitable transfer vacancies he shall be declared redundant. He shall be entitled to a period of notice as set down under the heading

Compensation below in addition to a redundancy payment, the amount to be determined by the provisions of the Redundancy Payments Act, 1965. He shall not be entitled to supplementary unemployment benefit (as set down in paragraph 4 under the heading *Compensation* below) but has the right of appeal in accordance with the section on *Appeals*.

6 Should an employee be transferred to another location where it is necessary for him to move his home, he shall be entitled to the following benefits:

(*a*) Payment of the return fare for the transferring employee and one dependent, for them to acquaint themselves with their place of transfer.

(*b*) Payment of fares for the employee and all dependents permanently moving with him.

(*c*) Payment of the cost of moving the employee's furniture and personal effects.

(*d*) Payment of a "disturbance allowance" of one month's salary.

(*e*) Payment of hotel bills up to £2 each a night for the employee and one dependent for a maximum period of five months after transfer has been effected.

(*f*) Guarantees to be given by the company to a building society to assist transferring employees in obtaining mortgages for house purchase.

7 Should an employee unreasonably refuse transfer opportunities, his case will be dealt with under paragraph 5 above. An employee who refuses to move his home as a result of being transferred shall *not* be deemed to have unreasonably refused a suitable transfer vacancy.

8 Any employee who is transferred shall be given particulars, in writing, of the terms and conditions of his new job. These particulars shall include a clear idea of:

(*a*) What other work is being offered.

(*b*) Its location.

(*c*) The rate of pay, including intervals at which it is paid.

(*d*) The normal hours of work.

(*e*) Holiday entitlements.

(*f*) Any special conditions relating to sickness or injury.

(*g*) Pension entitlement.

(*h*) The amount of notice required by both employer and employee.

Other measures to avoid redundancy

1   Whenever the company anticipates that redundancy may occur, it will halt any work which may, at the time, be sub-contracted, and will allocate this work to the department where redundancy threatens, always provided that this is technically feasible and economically realistic.

2   Whenever the company anticipates that redundancy may occur, and *some or all* of the measures to deal with this situation (already referred to in this plan) have been applied, overtime shall be reduced or shall cease, where this is feasible

3   Whenever the company anticipates that redundancy may occur and *all* measures to deal with this situation (already referred to in this plan) have been applied, the company will investigate the possibility of short-time working in the department affected.

Dismissal criteria

1   Where all other measures (already referred to in this plan) are insufficient to deal with the problem, redundancy may take place.

2   When employees are to be declared redundant, their selection shall take place in the following order:

(*a*) Male employees over the age of 65. Female employees over the age of 60.

(*b*) Part-time workers normally working less than twenty-one hours weekly.

(*c*) Volunteers.

(*d*) Married women with husbands working.

(*e*) Male employees over the age of 55; female employees over the age of 50, provided that they have completed sufficient service to entitle them to a pension.

(*f*) Short-service employees in preference to long-service employees, all other things being equal.

Periods of warning and notice

1   A period of warning is the notification by the company to a group of employees that redundancy will take place amongst their numbers.

217

2   A period of notice, on the other hand, is given to the affected individuals and gives a date on which his employment will be terminated.

3   In the event of potential redundancy the company will give employees as long a period of warning as possible, but not less than six weeks. This period shall be extended in the case of mass redundancy. (See *Additional measures in the case of mass redundancy* on page 222.)

4   The period of notice shall be given in addition to the period of warning (as set out above) and will be six weeks in addition to the notice as required by the provisions of the Contracts of Employment Act, 1963.

Compensation

1   All employees who are declared redundant by the Company shall be entitled to a redundancy payment, provided that:
   (*a*) They have completed more than two years' service.
   (*b*) They are aged over 20 but under 65 (60 for women).
   (*c*) They are normally working more than twenty-one hours weekly.
   (*d*) They have not been recruited temporarily on a fixed term contract.

2   The amount of redundancy payment shall be determined by the Redundancy Payments Act, 1965.

3   The company will give all redundant employees a written statement detailing how the amount of their redundancy payment has been calculated. The statement shall be given to the employee as soon as possible after notice has been given but in any case before employment is terminated.

4   Further financial assistance will be given to redundant employees unable to obtain other suitable employment, except:
   (*a*) Employees with under two years' service.
   (*b*) Employees aged under 20 and over 65 (60 for women).
   (*c*) Employees normally working less than twenty-one hours weekly.
   (*d*) Married women with husbands working;
   (*e*) Employees who unreasonably refuse transfer opportunities. (See the sub-section "transfer" under *Measures to avoid redundancy* on page 217.)

(*f*) Employees who have been temporarily recruited on fixed term contracts.

—and provided that:

(*g*) They have registered as unemployed at the local office of the Department of Employment and Productivity, as confirmed by the payment of national insurance unemployment benefit.

(*h*) They do not refuse suitable alternative employment in such a way as to disqualify them from receiving national insurance unemployment benefit.

(*i*) The company has no other evidence that the employee is not genuinely seeking other work.

5   This further financial assistance will take the form of supplementary unemployment benefit and will be at the rate of one-third of a week's basic wage or salary.

6   The maximum period for which the company will pay supplementary unemployment benefit is twenty-six weeks.

7   Married women not paying into the unemployment benefit fund, and therefore not in receipt of national insurance unemployment benefit, must furnish the company with a certificate that they have registered with the employment exchange and are genuinely seeking work.

8   Any employee who leaves the company's employment before receiving notice (*not* warning) of his termination of employment shall not be entitled to a redundancy payment or supplementary unemployment benefit.

Appeals

1   Any employee who believes that either:

(*a*) He has been unfairly declared redundant (with due regard to the provisions of this plan;

(*b*) That his treatment has been unfair in terms of the compensation and notice he is entitled to receive under this plan;

—shall have the right to appeal to a redundancy appeals committee.

2   The redundancy appeals committee shall consist of:

(*a*) A shop steward or member of the staff committee selected by the appellant in the department where he is normally employed.

(*b*) The senior shop steward of the employee's trade union in the factory or the chairman of the staff committee.

(*c*) The personnel manager.

(*d*) An executive director.

3   All decisions of the redundancy appeals committee are final and must be unanimous.

Assistance in finding work

1   Every effort will be made by the company to assist redundant employees in obtaining suitable alternative employment.

2   In particular, the company will:

(*a*) Contact other employers in the area to ascertain whether they have any suitable vacancies.

(*b*) Inform the local office of the Department of Employment and Productivity *at least* fourteen days before any dismissals are to take effect. This period shall be increased to twenty-eight days where ten or more employees are to be declared redundant simultaneously.

Preferential re-engagement rights

Any employee who has been declared redundant by the company shall have preference over other applicants for re-employment by the company, provided that he had completed one year's satisfactory service prior to having been declared redundant.

Additional measures in the case of mass redundancy

In the case of mass redundancy—that is, affecting fifty or more workers or 10 per cent or more of the labour force in a factory of the company—the following additional measures will be taken:

1   The minimum period of warning shall be increased to twelve weeks, and individual workers shall be informed of their impending redundancy at least three weeks prior to receiving notice.

2   The Department of Employment and Productivity will be invited to send one of its officials to the factory concerned to discuss employment opportunities. In special cases the Department may set up its own office on the company's premises.

Consultation

The company will inform the appropriate trade unions as soon as it is seen that redundancy will take place, and will discuss with them the measures it intends to take to deal with the situation.

Miscellaneous provisions

1   The company reserves the right to recruit temporary labour in order to ensure a smooth transition to new processes or methods where this is applicable. The company recognises, however, that its first responsibility is, and will remain, towards its permanent full-time employees.

2   The provisions of this employment security plan supersede all previous policy statements on redundancy for both staff and hourly paid employees.

Recommended Constitution for a Works Productivity Council

The primary aim of the works productivity council shall be to increase the prosperity of the company and its employees. It is created in the belief that the whole of the company's resources should be mobilised to this end, that the exchange of ideas is necessary to both sides, that discussion is the mature and businesslike way of achieving this end, that the men and women employed by the company have knowledge and skills which can make a significant contribution to the solving of problems which arise on the shop floor.

Objects and Scope

The chairman of the council shall take decisions to further these ends in the light of discussion in the following broadly defined areas:

Exchange of information

1   Information from management on factory performance on new projects, new work, immediate work-load and programming.
2   Review of recent performances in the light of targets set, and discussion of any measures taken or to be taken for rectification and improvement.
3   Information from representatives on problem areas experienced and snags to be expected.
4   Feed-back of information on recent improvements and review of their effectiveness.

Suggestions

Suggestions from representatives for economic improvements in:

1 Method of working.
2 Techniques and machinery.
3 Use of materials.
4 General factory housekeeping.
5 Conditions of working, including heating, ventilation, lighting, cleanliness, hygiene and accident prevention.
6 Training of men, women and juveniles.
7 Manning of lines and machines and distribution of work.
8 Absenteeism.

Appeals procedure

An appeals procedure has been specially instituted to deal with matters of a personal nature. Where an individual has an appeal or grievance which he wishes to draw to the attention of his manager he should use this procedure. For this reason personal grievances are excluded from the discussion of committees.

Matters outside the council's competence

Provision for discussion of the following matters are made through separate channels, and they are therefore excluded from the discussions of the council:

1 Matters which are subject of a national agreement or which are normally decided by direct negotiations between the senior representatives of the trade unions and the employers' federation (examples of these are the basic rates of pay and the length of the normal working week). Such matters are dealt with initially by management and trades unions in accordance with the agreed procedure for settling disputes. (See Appendix 11.)
2 Matters of a personal nature, where an individual has an appeal or grievance which he wishes to draw to the attention of his manager. These matters are settled through the appeals procedure. (See Appendix 10.)

3   Suggestions not affecting the whole factory and made by individuals for consideration by the suggestion awards committee of the council. (See Appendix 9.) Suggestions are referred to the chairman of the suggestions awards committee who, if he decides they have implications affecting the rest of the factory, may refer the suggestion to the council for wider discussion.

Membership

Ex officio

Chief executive, personnel manager, senior shop steward or convenor of all major unions.

Nominated

Representative of senior and junior management—non-union members.

Officers

Chairman: general manager.
Secretary: elected by the council from within its number.

Co-option

At the chairman's discretion, the council may co-opt to particular meetings persons whose knowledge will contribute to the solution of a problem or problems which have been placed before it.

Deputies

Where a member of the council is unable to attend a meeting, he may nominate a deputy to attend in his place. The deputy must have a clear and full brief from his representative and may commit him to any decision to which the deputy is party. Should an elected member be unable to attend the council for three meetings in succession, the council should offer his constituents an opportunity of electing a representative to replace him (see also *Casual vacancies* below).

Minutes

The secretary shall take minutes of the decisions taken in council. Draft minutes shall be submitted to the chairman for his approval before circulation. These should be posted on the factory notice boards within two days of the meeting they record. They should be brief and crisp but give sufficient indication of the discussion to make sense to persons not attending the meeting. Copies should be circulated to all foremen and staff section leaders and to those concerned in matters raised.

Agenda

Before each meeting, the secretary should approach members of the council, compile from them an agenda, submit it to the chairman for approval and post it not later than two working days before that meeting. The chairman has the authority to exclude from discussion items which have not been specified on the published agenda.

Time

Initially, meetings should be held once a month and a time limit of one and a half hours' maximum duration should be set by the chairman.

Expenses

The cost of secretarial services and administrative expenses shall be borne by the company. Representatives shall be adequately reimbursed for earnings lost whilst attending a meeting of the council.

Elections

Elections shall be held every year except for casual vacancies which are covered under *Casual vacancies* below. It is the executive responsibility of the company secretary to ensure that elections are conducted in the proper manner.

List of electors

Not less than one month before the date of an election, the company secretary shall post in each constituency a list of employees who may vote in that constituency. Any errors or omissions brought to the notice of the company secretary not later than the Saturday prior to the election shall be rectified. Thereafter, the list shall be regarded as definitive.

Nominations

Due notice shall be given that nominations are required. The deadline and place of receipt shall be stated. A nominee must signify his willingness to stand by signing a standard form at the request of his proposer and seconders who must also sign.

Voting

Voting shall be by ballot. No voter should be permitted to cast his vote except in person and during the defined hours of voting. An arrangement for "postal voting" should be made for those employees who are unable to vote in person owing to:

1   Absence on holiday.
2   Instructions to work in some other place.
3   Suspension.
4   Shift requirements.

Election should be by simple majority in the first instance. In the event of a tie, a further election must be held between the candidates who tied. In the event of a second tie, length of service with the company as defined for the Contracts of Employment Act shall determine the choice.

The declaration of the company secretary as to the validity of any voting papers and on the counting of votes shall be final, except that a recount may be demanded by a consensus of at least half of the electors.

Notice of the results of the elections should be posted by the company secretary within one working day of the close of voting. Voting slips should be destroyed before witnesses after the first meeting of the council.

Casual vacancies

If a representative leaves the company, is transferred from his unit, resigns from his duties as a representative or is required by a majority of his electorate to resign, notice of the vacancy should be posted in his constituency and nominations invited in the manner described above. A successor should be elected within a month of the occurrances of the vacancy. A representative elected to fill a casual vacancy should serve until the next annual election.

Discretionary matters

The council has powers to discuss rules for the conduct of its affairs within this general pattern. Items not covered which the council may wish to define for itself are:

Canvassing.
Qualifications of nominees and electors.
Quorums.
Penalties for non-attendance.
Dismissal of representatives by electors.

Major alterations to the constitution of the council require the sanction of the board of directors.

Relationship between productivity committees and the works productivity council

Each productivity committee may choose from its elected representatives one member who shall attend the works productivity council to speak on their behalf.

The constitution of the works productivity council is set out previously. The two constitutions are similar; the main difference between the two bodies is in the scope of discussion. The works productivity council is constituted primarily for discussion of matters which affect the whole or a major part of the company, whereas productivity committees are constituted to discuss matters of immediate concern to their own department. Matters affecting the whole company may be raised at productivity committees but where the chairman has no authority to decide on such suggestions he may pass the matter on to his higher managers who may bring the matter up to the works productivity council.

Notes for the Guidance of Committee Chairmen, Representatives and Electors

The following notes, which may be taken in conjunction with Appendix 7, are intended for the guidance of those who serve on committees as chairmen or representatives, and of those who elect representatives. A company's system of communications and consultation can never be effective unless all concerned know their responsibilities.

Chairmen

Productivity committees should be used to sift and settle matters which are of concern to the department only, and to eliminate from the works council matters which would be regarded by other departments as trivial or unrewarding in general discussion. Where matters of a general nature are brought up, the superintendent should refer them to his higher manager up the executive chain, having ascertained the views of his representatives and clarified with them the proposals which they have for improving the matter. If the matter is resolved by his higher manager, he must then report this back to his committee. There will be matters on which such solutions are unsatisfactory to the representatives. Where these matters are considered large enough for consideration by the works council, either party may put them on the agenda for discussion.

It should be recognised from the start that this type of discussion is an *appeal* against managerial policy. It is therefore up to managers, first, to clarify policies amongst themselves and *commit* their managerial subordinates to their policies before they are further discussed with the representatives. In this way the insidious position of a manager using his work-force to give backing to what is essentially his own appeal is minimised, and the fatal type of situation is avoided in which a manager reports back to his committee that "well, I tried but *they* decided it couldn't be done." He must realise that, if he is not committed to what his manager decides, he must tackle his manager until he gets satisfaction with a policy he can commit himself to, or leave his job (it is as simple as that).

Secondly, it is up to managers to decide whether it is necessary to consult on the matter. Consultation needs to be held on matters where sanction is needed—in matters, that is, where the strength of resistance to a policy seems to be strong and needs to be gauged more accurately. It is this aspect of the communications network which is of great value to a general manager: it functions as a sounding board to tell him just how far he can go with his subordinates.

Representatives

A representative is accountable to the constituency which elects him. It is his responsibility to:

1 Make himself aware of the main interests of all in his constituency.

2 Represent the point of view of his constituents, even where this may mean presenting a point of view contrary to his own personal opinion.

3 Assist his constituents to arrive at a consensus or reconsider it by giving information and advice based on his experience or knowledge of company policy and procedures and on his knowledge of management attitude and opinion.

4 Present the consensus of his constituents, avoiding the identification of this consensus with any particular individuals.

5 Allow committees and council to work with the greatest possible realism by judging when to state any minority views held within his constituency or committee.

6 Judge when he should refer matters to his constituents and when to accept responsibility for acting without referring to them.

7 Initiate proposals for change which would be in the best interests of his constituents.

8 Take appropriate steps when, in his judgement, the actions of his managers or the actions of his constituents are inconsistent with known policy.

9 Assist his constituents to understand how the agreements he has accepted on their behalf will affect them at work.

10 Familiarise himself with the rules and procedures of the committees or council on which he sits.

11 Know the policy of the company, and particularly the stated policy which is of immediate concern to his constituents.

12 Ensure before taking up a matter with and on behalf of his constituents that the constituent has in the first instance taken the matter up with his manager.

Electors

A constituent or elector has certain rights and responsibilities:

1 He has the right to participate in the election of his representative in accordance with the rules which are set down.

2 He should co-operate with his representative and his fellow electors in deciding the general lines to be followed by his representative in committee or council.

3 He should, as far as is possible, allow his representative full authority to speak for him and consider himself bound by any agreement to which his representative commits him.

4 He must accept the consequences of not keeping himself informed about those aspects of company policy which are likely to affect him.

5 He should pass to his representative any information which will enable the representative to act in full awareness of the main interest of his constituents. Trade union interests, where they exist, will be included in this category.

6 He may seek advice on matters to do with his employment and his work at any time, but may only seek action through his representative if he has first taken the matter up with his foreman or section leader and has been unable after a reasonable time, to obtain satisfaction.

Recommended Constitution for a Suggestion Scheme

Policy

The suggestions scheme is intended to encourage all employees to put forward ideas concerning the improvement of production, the devising of new methods, reducing costs as a result of delays, increasing efficiency, eliminating waste and duplication, conserving time and materials and preventing accidents.

Administration

The suggestions scheme will be administered by the suggestion awards committee of the works productivity council. The committee shall consist of:

> *Ex officio*: the cost controller (chairman) and a shop superintendent.
> *Elected*: two representatives elected from the number of the council.

The duties of the committee shall be:

1   To receive and briefly record all notifications of suggestions, the decisions taken on each, and the awards made for those which are successful.

2   To take up each individual suggestion with the person submitting it and his foreman or manager, and assist him in

exploring the feasibility, cost and acceptability of the suggestion and its implications for the rest of the factory.

3 Where the chairman of the committee decides that the suggestion has implications which would involve the rest of the factory, he may refer the suggestion to general discussion in the works productivity council.

4 The committee shall ensure that a clear decision is made by the appropriate manager as to whether the suggestion is accepted or not, and ensure that the person submitting the suggestion is aware of the decision and the reasons for it.

5 The committee shall see to it that no undue delay is made in a decision being taken.

6 Where a suggestion is accepted, the committee shall monitor progress on implementation.

7 Where a suggestion is accepted the committee shall report the fact to the managing director and recommend to him an appropriate award within the guiding figures set by him.

8 The chairman of the committee is responsible for ensuring sound publicity to the scheme, encouraging suggestions and ensuring that the scheme does not fall into disrepute.

Rules of the scheme

Eligibility

1 All employees may participate in the scheme.

2 There are no limitations on the number of suggestions made or awards given.

Anonymity

In normal circumstances, a person making a suggestion would be expected to be prepared to discuss it openly; but if, for special reasons, he wishes to remain anonymous, he may meet a member of the committee in private and arrange for him to present the details of his suggestion to the committee for him.

Awards

Awards for successful suggestions will be made within guiding figures set by the managing director. Under the present arrangements, the Inland Revenue authorities are prepared to treat awards as non-taxable in cases where it can be shown that the suggestion was made outside the normal course of duties.

Method of making a suggestion

Suggestion notification slips will be available in all departments adjacent to a collection box. An example of the notification slip is shown in Figure A9:1. The slip is not intended for recording the full details of the suggestion: it is intended to serve as a notification to the committee that the person filling in the slip would like to discuss his ideas more fully.

```
                      NOTIFICATION OF SUGGESTION

    Name (print)_____     Submission date_____

    Clock number_____     Department_____


    To the Chairman, Suggestion Awards Committee
    Please note that I would like to discuss with
    you a suggestion I have about_____
    _____
    _____

                                    Signature_____



    Note: If you wish your name to be kept confidential tick
          here [    ] and put this slip in an envelope before
          posting it in the box
```

FIGURE A9:1   EXAMPLE OF A NOTIFICATION SLIP

A person wishing to put forward a suggestion fills in a notification slip and drops it into the collection box.

If a person making a suggestion wishes to remain anonymous, he should put his name on the slip but place the slip in an envelope before posting it in the collection box.

The chairman of the suggestion awards committee must arrange for the collection boxes to be cleared daily. He must acknowledge receipt immediately.

Record of suggestions

Each suggestion received will be recorded in a book or file kept by the chairman of the suggestion awards committee under the following headings:

233

1 Date of suggestion.
2 Name of suggester.
3 Clock number.
4 Department.
5 Brief details of suggestion.
6 Action taken.
7 Agreement to accept or reject.
8 Suggester informed (date).
9 Manager implementing.
10 Award.

Notification slips will be retained and filed alphabetically under the name of the suggester.

Adjudication of suggestions

Suggestions received will be taken up by the awards committee and the suggester with the manager who is empowered to decide on the matter covered by the suggestion. He will make a decision in the light of discussion with the suggester and the committee. In cases of disagreement with his decision, the appeals procedure may be invoked.

Discoveries and inventions

Suggestions can only be considered on condition that if they consist of, or include, any discovery or invention:

1 The right of the discovery or invention will belong to the company.
2 The suggester who conceived the discovery or invention will, at the request of the company assign to the company, free of charge, his title to the discovery or invention and will do everything necessary to give effect to the assignment and to enable the company to secure patent protection for the discovery or invention in any country or countries.

Payment of awards

When a recommendation is approved by the managing director, details of the award should be passed to the company secretary for payment.

Notable awards should be made personally and publicly to the suggester by a director of the company. An appropriate time and place for such a presentation would be in the canteen during a lunch break.

Recommended Appeals Procedure

Appeals procedure—general

When an employee objects to a decision of his immediate superior, he may challenge that decision if he feels it is out of line with the company's policy, unfair, biased or prejudiced by generally accepted standards. The appeal shall be referred by the superior to the next highest person in the management chain if he cannot settle the matter himself. The appellant should be allowed to call in an advisor of his own choosing. If the appellant receives a decision on the case from his manager-once-removed which he again feels is not in accord with company policy or unfair, he is able to appeal against the manager's decision to the next highest level. If agreement is not reached at this stage an appeals inquiry shall be conducted by the personnel manager, whose decision shall be final.

When groups of employees have grievances of a similar nature against a common manager's decision, they should have the right to appoint a spokesman to conduct their appeal up the chain of management against successive decisions, as above. Managers should hear appeals within a reasonable period after official notification of the appeal. The final decision is that of the company chief executive.

It should be the executive responsibility of the personnel manager to ensure that this appeals policy is carried out and does not fall into disrepute. The following procedures should apply:

1   A standard notice of appeal (in triplicate) should be made available to all managers.

2   If an appellant feels that after three working days insufficient action has been taken by his manager to deal with his appeal,

he may request the manager to complete the notification form. Both manager and appellant sign the form, which is then sent to the personnel manager. No manager may refuse this request.

3 The original is retained by the manager and a copy is sent to the personnel manager. The second copy is retained by the manager until the appeal has been heard. Having heard the appeal, the manager enters details of the resulting decision on his copy and on the original. The second copy is then sent to the personnel manager.

Timing of appeals

Appeals shall be heard by managers within a reasonable period from the formal notification of the appeal by the appellant.

If an employee intends to give notification of an appeal, he must do so within three working days of the giving of the instruction against which he is appealing.

Where an appellant feels that, after three working days, insufficient action has been taken by his manager to deal with his appeal he may request his manager to inform the works director (or his deputy) of the situation. A manager may not refuse this request.

Whilst an appeal is pending, work shall proceed in the normal manner and the instruction against which the appeal is made shall be carried out.

Responsibility for procedure

It is the executive responsibility of the works director to ensure that this appeals procedure is carried out and does not fall into disrepute.

Emergencies

Where the works director feels that an appeal is likely to cause severe damage to morale if it is not dealt with immediately, he may convene a meeting at which are present the appellant(s) his (their) representative, the supervisor directly concerned and all the intermediate managers in the direct executive chain between that supervisor and himself. He will then investigate the situation and decide whether to give an immediate decision or allow the appeal to proceed through the set channels.

Procedure for appeals on standards and job rates

Where an employee or group of employees does not accept a standard or an alteration to a standard or job rate which applies to them, the following procedure will apply. The disputed standard or job rate will be discussed with the appropriate rate fixer in the presence of the foreman. If agreement is not reached, the appropriate representatives—including one knowledgeable in the methods of setting standards and rates—will discuss the standard or job rate with their superintendent and the rate fixer. If agreement is still not reached, a trial run superintended by the cost controller or his deputy, and in the presence of the experienced employee representative, shall take place and the results shall be reported back to the superintendent. If agreement is still not reached, the works director shall be informed and the procedure outlined above under *General appeals* followed.

During the hearing of an appeal, work will continue and the final decision will be applied retrospectively.

Recommended Procedure for Settling Disputes

This example of a disputes procedure in a manufacturing company derives from the *Handbook of National Agreements* for the engineering industry, as detailed below.

There is a nationally agreed procedure for settling disputes which is binding upon both unions and managements in this company. The full details of the procedure are set out in the *Handbook of National Agreements*, reference 1–1.2 under the heading "Procedure: manual workers, (2) Provisions for avoiding disputes." The steps in the procedure may be summarised as below. Where a question of dispute arises over the application of:

1   General alterations in wages.
2   Alterations in working conditions which are the subject of agreements officially entered into.
3   Alterations in the general working week.

An endeavour must be made by the management and workmen concerned to settle the matter themselves at the factory. The procedure at this stage is as follows:

1   The man concerned must first take up the matter with his foreman.
2   If this fails, he may request his shop steward to take the matter up for him with the foreman.

3   If the foreman and the shop steward fail to agree they take the matter before the foreman's manager (normally the shop superintendent).

4   If this fails, the shop steward and the manager take the matter to the next manager (normally the works director). When the matter reaches the level of works director, a full meeting of all shop stewards with management representatives is called.

If this fails, the works conference must be called to discuss the matter further. At a works conference the workmen concerned, or their representatives, may be accompanied by their organiser. If the organiser is present a representative from the employers' federation must be present on the management side.

If the works conference does not solve the disagreement, either party may call for a local conference on the matter. A local conference is conducted by their organiser (for the trade union) and the representative of the employers' federation (for the management). A local conference must be held within seven days of notification unless otherwise agreed.

If the local conference fails to solve the disagreement, either side may call for a central conference to recommend a solution. Central conferences are conducted at ——— on the second Friday of each month by senior representatives of both organisations.

Until this procedure is carried through, there must be no stoppage of work either of a partial or a general character.

Proposals for a Productivity Agreement

A checklist of the likely components of a comprehensive productivity agreement is shown below.

Specimen contents

INTRODUCTION

SECTION I: APPRAISAL OF THE PRESENT SITUATION

SECTION II: PROPOSED NEW WAGES SYSTEM

1   General principles.
2   Basic rate.
3   Direct incentive element.
4   Indirect incentive element.
5   Method of payment.
6   Annual improvement factor.
7   Premium payments.
8   Payment levels: female employees and youths under twenty-one.
9   Allowances and special conditions payments.
10 Introduction of the system.
11 Benefits from the proposals.

SECTION III: CHANGES IN WORKING PRACTICES

1   General principles.
2   Hours of work.

(*a*) Reduction in overtime.
(*b*) Rationalisation of shift systems.
3   Increased flexibility and mobility of labour.
4   Limitations to full labour utilisation.
5   Methods of measurement: review of standards.

SECTION IV: DISCIPLINARY PROCEDURES

1   Basic principles.
2   Timekeeping and attendance standards.
3   Tea-breaks.
4   Breaches of discipline.
5   Dismissal.
6   Appeals procedure.

SECTION V: COMMUNICATIONS STRUCTURE

1   Procedure agreement.
2   Negotiating structure.
3   Advisory structure.
4   Appeals system.

SECTION VI: SECURITY OF EMPLOYMENT PLAN

1   Introduction.
2   Measures to avoid redundancy.
3   Dismissal criteria.
4   Periods of warning and notice.
5   Compensation.
6   Appeals.
7   Assistance in finding other work.
8   Preferential re-engagement rights.
9   Additional measures in the case of a large redundancy.
10   Consultation.

SECTION VII: PROGRAMME OF IMPLEMENTATION

1   Programme of introduction of payment schemes.
2   Provisions for interim payments.

Productivity Agreement and New System of Wage Payment

The following is from an actual company booklet

This booklet is important, and we hope it will be read by every employee. It describes the important parts of the productivity agreement and new system of wage payment which is being negotiated with your representatives.

The agreement will affect everybody in the works. It will mean change and better employment conditions and wage rates; it will mean shorter hours, more shift working and increased efficiency.

When it is negotiated and fully operative, it will make the company a more interesting place to work in and will enable us to meet the challenges of increased competition.

So please read the following pages carefully, and ask your foreman or shop steward if there is anything that is not clear or if you want fuller details.

Productivity agreement

Why has this agreement been negotiated?

For some time, management and employees have wanted to improve and simplify the wage system. As a result, the job evaluation programme was carried out. Consultants helped us to prepare the proposals for negotiation. These proposals are designed to improve wage rates and raise productivity to pay for these higher wages— and at the same time, reduce our costs of production and thereby make ourselves more competitive.

What improvements will this agreement produce?

When the agreement is operating fully, the wage rates of employees will increase on average by over 19 per cent. The improved efficiency to be obtained from the agreement will raise the productivity of the works by at least 25 per cent and will allow us to increase our share of world markets, thereby ensuring greater security of employment.

What is increased productivity?

Increased productivity means either:

1   More produced by employees in the same time, or
2   The same amount produced in a shorter time.

Each of these ways will be used at these works to obtain higher productivity but, in general, this agreement will lead to shorter hours for many employees at higher hourly rates of pay.

What does the agreement include?

The agreement includes:

1   A completely new and simplified wage system.
2   Changes in working methods and practices.
3   Changes in employment standards.
4   Proposals for full joint consultation.
5   A detailed security-of-employment plan.
6   A defined promotion structure.

Wage system

What are the proposals for the new wage system?

The new wage system consists of three parts:

1   *A basic rate.* Five grades have been established by job evaluation. Each of these grades has a separate basic rate, and the five rates will cover all employees. Your foreman or shop steward can tell you into which grade your job falls.
2   *A direct incentive.* This will be paid to all employees whose work, either as an individual or as a member of a gang or small group, can be accurately measured. The bonus paid will reward your effort and application.
3   *An indirect incentive.* This bonus will be paid to every employee

in the works. It will reward the co-operation, flexibility and willingness of employees. It will be measured by the productivity of the main areas of the works.

How much is the basic rate?

You will find the basic rates for each grade in the tables at the back of the booklet. (See Figure A13:1.) The basic rate will amount to three-quarters (75 per cent) of the earnings of employees whose work is measured when working at standard rate. For employees whose work is not directly measured, the basic rate will be four-fifths (80 per cent) of earnings at standard rate.

What will the basic rate be used for?

It will be used for the payment of all attendance hours at the factory even if work is not available. It will also be the basis on which the incentives are calculated. It will *not* be used to calculate premiums, overtime or holiday pay, which will be based on national agreements.

What are the proposals for the direct incentive?

The direct incentive bonus will be paid according to the performance of individuals or small groups. Performance will be measured by the most appropriate techniques, for instance, work measurement. We expect that, on average, these employees will be able to earn one-fifth (20 per cent) of their basic rate under this part of the wage system. This average amount of money will vary according to the grade of the employee. The amount of bonus for standard performance are shown in the tables at the back of the booklet. (See Figure A13:1.)

What are the proposals for the indirect incentive?

The indirect incentive will be based on the overall performance, measured over four separate areas of the works:

1   Large finishing, small finishing and drawbench departments.
2   Fine finishing department.
3   Forging department.
4   Pilger mill

The overall performance of an area will determine the bonus levels for employees. Performance is measured by an index which improves when the productivity of the area or areas goes up, that is, more is produced in a shorter time.

	Job grade	Consolidated time rate (CTR)	Basic rate	DIRECT WORKERS			INDIRECT WORKERS		Job specification
				Individual bonus	Department bonus	Total earnings	Department bonus	Total earnings	
1 hour 40 hours	A	£10–6–0	78·9d £13–3–0	15·8d £2–12–6	10·5d £1–15–2	105·2d £17–10–8	15·8d £2–12–6	94·7d £15–15–6	Semi-skilled
1 hour 40 hours	B	£10–6–0	85·3d £14–4–4	17·0d £2–16–8	11·4d £1–18–0	113·7d £18–19–0	17·0d £2–16–8	102·3d £17–1–0	Semi-skilled
1 hour 40 hours	C	£10–6–0	93·2d £15–10–8	18·6d £3–2–2	12·4d £2–1–4	124·2d £20–14–2	18·6d £3–2–2	111·8d £18–12–10	Semi-skilled
1 hour 40 hours	D	£10–6–0	102·2d £17–0–8	20·4d £3–8–0	13·7d £2–5–8	136·3d £22–14–4	20·4d £3–8–0	122·6d £20–8–8	Semi-skilled
1 hour 40 hours	E	£10–6–0	112·5d £18–15–0	22·5d £3–15–0	15·0d £2–10–0	150·0d £25–0–0	22·5d £3–15–0	135·0d £22–10–0	Semi-skilled
1 hour 40 hours	EX	£11–9–8	112·5d £18–15–0	22·5d £3–15–0	15·0d £2–10–0	150·0d £25–0–0	22·5d £3–15–0	135·0d £22–10–0	Skilled maintenance

FIGURE A13:1   WAGE STRUCTURE: BUILD UP OF EARNINGS

The index takes account of differences in the products and will go up when everybody in an area works as a team and co-operates with each other to the full. At a 100 per cent performance, the amount of this incentive bonus will be $13\frac{1}{2}$ per cent of basic rate for those covered by the direct incentive and 20 per cent of basic rate for indirect workers.

What is this indirect incentive trying to achieve?

This part of the wage system is designed to pay employees for the use of *all* their abilities, not just their efforts. It will promote team work, flexibility, ideas and suggestions; it will also encourage those in each work area to work together constructively to produce high quality products at maximum yield. Management and supervision will also be seeking to obtain maximum efficiency.

Annual improvement factor

What is the annual improvement factor?

This is a means whereby employees can share in the prosperity of the company. Where, through all-round improvement, the cost of labour fall in proportion to other major costs (excluding raw materials) a share of the savings will be applied to basic rates. This will be done annually, provided the targets set up are achieved. This will be more fully explained to everyone at a later date.

Method of payment

What changes are proposed for the payment of wages?

These changes are important because they are designed to give employees a more stable pay packet each week.

How is this stability achieved?

In two ways. First, employees' performances under the incentive parts of the wage system will be averaged over a monthly period. The average performance for one monthly period will establish the level of pay for the next month.

Second, the direct and indirect incentive bonuses will be paid in increments related to bands of performance. You will find these bands in the tables at the back of the booklet. (See Figure A13:2.) Against each band an amount of bonus will be paid, according to which grade the employee's job is in. The higher the band, the higher the bonus. The bands are quite wide, so small variations in performance will not alter the amount of money paid.

Job grade	Performance range / Payband	Up to 85 / 1	82–95 / 2	92–105 / 3	102–115 / 4	112 and over / 5
A	1 hour 40 hours	3·2d 10s 8d	9·5d £1–11–8	15·8d £2–12–8	22·1d £3–13–8	28·4d £4–14–8
B	1 hour 40 hours	3·4d 11s 4d	10·2d £1–14–0	17·0d £2–16–8	23·8d £3–19–4	30·6d £5–2–0
C	1 hour 40 hours	3·7d 12s 4d	11·2d £1–17–4	18·6d £3–2–0	26·0d £4–6–8	33·5d £5–11–8
D	1 hour 40 hours	4·1d 13s 8d	12·2d £2–0–8	20·4d £3–8–0	28·6d £4–15–4	36·7d £6–2–4
E	1 hour 40 hours	4·5d 15s 0d	13·5d £2–5–0	22·5d £3–15–0	31·5d £5–5–0	40·5d £6–15–0

FIGURE A13:2   WAGE STRUCTURE: INDIVIDUAL BONUS PAY BANDS (*a, b, c*)

Premium payment and allowances

What are the arrangements for the payment of premiums and holidays?

As already mentioned, payments for overtime and holidays will be based on national agreements and will be improved from 1 January. There are special payments for working shifts.

What are these payments for shift work?

Shift premiums for two and three eight-hour shift working will be calculated on rates well in excess of those nationally agreed and using overtime premiums, when required, as laid down in the engineering agreement. A similar basis will be used for continuous shift working in the maintenance departments, coupled with an additional disturbance allowance.

What allowances will be paid?

The only allowance to be paid in future will be a "hot working allowance" of 1*s* (5*p*) an hour. This will be paid to employees who, for more than 75 per cent of their shift, work within 10 feet (3 m) of an open furnace or work-piece at a temperature in excess of 1000°C and are exposed to the radiant heat. Re-evaluation of jobs in receipt of this allowance will be necessary.

What about waiting time?

Periods of time beyond employees' control, when they are unable to continue on productive work, will be paid at that basic rate plus the indirect incentive bonus.

Other provisions on wages

The productivity agreement contains detailed arrangements covering:

1   Transfers.
2   Trainees.
3   Sub-standard work.
4   Protection of earnings awards.

You can learn about these details by asking your foreman or shop steward.

Changes in working practices and employment standards

What are the main changes included in the productivity agreement?

The agreement includes detailed proposals to improve productivity in respect of:

1   Hours of work.
2   Job enlargement and flexibility of labour.
3   Employment standards and conditions—for example, absenteeism, timekeeping, tea breaks.

What changes in hours of work are proposed in the agreement?

Basically, systematic overtime is to be abolished and overtime worked only when really necessary. It is a declared intention of the agreements to cut down the long hours many employees have been asked to work in recent years. It is also proposed to increase the amount of shift working and to simplify the shift system which are worked in the factory.

What are the shift systems going to be?

The following shift systems will be those primarily used:

248

1   Double day shift.
2   Rotating three shifts.
3   Rotating four shifts (probably confined to maintenance departments).

The normal day shift will also feature in the shift systems, but the permanent night shift will be replaced by other systems.

What is job enlargement?

The simplified five-grade structure and higher basic and fall-back rates will permit increased flexibility and mobility of labour. In particular, an examination of the jobs which fall within a grade will be made by each department. Wherever possible, an employee will be trained in more than one job in his grade. It is for this, among other things, that the higher basic rates are being paid. Thus employees will be asked in a number of cases to increase their versatility in respect of the work they can undertake.

What about employment standards and conditions?

The agreement makes detailed provision for establishing fair and uniform standards to be observed, covering time-keeping and absenteeism. These are designed to make sure that everyone knows what is expected and that variations in the treatment of employees do not occur.

Everyone will be informed what the standards are when the agreement is signed, and details of the proposals are available from your shop steward and foreman.

Communications and joint consultation

Why are there proposals on a communications structure in the productivity agreement?

The success of the productivity agreement will depend upon how well employees understand the principles and aims of the company and how much co-operation there is. The proposals for a communications structure are to establish means whereby this understanding and co-operation are secured.

What are the main parts of the communications structure?

In each department there will be a departmental productivity panel which will have a number of employees' representatives as well as

249

members of management and supervision. These panels will discuss all matters related to increased productivity in the department and will review the progress of the indirect incentive. The panels will provide an opportunity for employees to comment on and contribute to the department's productive efficiency and make suggestions for improvement.

Each departmental productivity panel will send representatives to the works advisory council, which will review the progress of the works overall, discuss all important matters referred to it by the productivity panels and consider the works' performance in relation to the annual improvement factor.

Security of employment plan

Why is there a security-of-employment plan?

The company recognises that security of employment is one of the primary needs of working life. It therefore has included in the productivity agreement a carefully designed plan which ensures that redundancy will occur only as a last resort, after all measures to prevent it have been fully explored.

What are the most likely measures the company will take to avoid redundancy?

1   Curtail recruitment.
2   Transfers, which will include retraining where necessary.
3   Reduction of overtime.
4   Short-time working for a limited period.

If such measures do not succeed, on what basis will employees leave the company?

The selection of employees to leave the company will take place on the following basis:

1   Male employees over the age of 65; female employees over 60.
2   Volunteers.
3   Short-service employees in preference to long-service employees.

The plan provides for warning to be given additional to that established by law and sets up an appeal system for any employee who considers he has been unfairly treated.

Implementation of the agreement

When does the agreement come into effect?

A date from which the agreement will operate will be agreed with your representatives. All the general sections of the agreement will then come into force, and afterwards the new wage system will be introduced as quickly as possible. The large finishing department will be the first, where it will be introduced almost immediately.

It is planned to cover the whole works within twelve months from the signature of the agreement, but the majority of the large departments will be covered in half this time.

Supervisors' Appreciation and Training Programme

An example of a training programme for supervisors designed to explain to them the objectives and purposes of a detailed productivity agreement, which is placed in the context of the business and related to their jobs. Details of the sessions are as follows.

1 *The company*   *45 minutes*

The structure and aims of the company—its relationship to the group. Current market position—changes envisaged and problems to be overcome. The importance of the customer.

2 *The works—present and future*   *60 minutes*

Present works performance—the need for reorganisation based on job definition and performance criteria. The provision of control information—the need to integrate the company and line management (including supervision).

3 *The role of the supervisor* (discussion)   *90 minutes*

Responsibilities and duties—how these are satisfactorily discharged —what the supervisor needs to know and what should be expected of him.

4   *Work study*   *90 minutes*

What is work study/method study/work measurement. Techniques
used and their application. Value to the company and effect on the
supervisor's job.

5   *Productivity and costs* (panel and discussion)   *90 minutes*

What is productivity? Present levels of productivity. How productivity can be improved and implications on company costs. The
supervisor's responsibility for productivity.

6   *The revised wage structure*   *60 minutes*

The existing wage structure and the need for revision. Principles on
which new structure is based. Proposals (short-term): grade structure
and departmental incentives; proposals (long-term): direct incentives
and establishment of a three-tier structure. Programme of implementation.

7   *Negotiation of agreement* (talk and discussion)   *60 minutes*

The aims of the productivity agreement. What an agreement should
cover. Main subjects included. Their implications for supervision.

8   *Motivation in industry*   *60 minutes*

Why people work; traditional views and their implications. More
recent findings—the need of individuals and how these may be
satisfied. How supervisors should motivate their subordinates.

9   *Communications* (discussion)   *90 minutes*

Why are communications necessary? What should be communicated
to employees and through what channels. A communications structure—command, negotiating and advisory. The foreman's responsibility for effective communication.

10   *Overcoming resistance to change* (film and syndicate work)
                                                          90 minutes

Supervisors would form syndicates to prepare suggestions of what
the implications of change will be for the employees and themselves
and how opposition can be overcome. [Syndicates should have an

opportunity for two further meetings before presenting their report in session 11.]

11 *Syndicate reports*   *60 minutes*
Discussion on the conclusions drawn.

12 *Summary of course and analysis of its results*   *30 minutes*
The immediate future for supervision.

Notes

Timing of the course

1   It is suggested that each course should be organised in half-day sessions of approximately three hours, arranged over a two-week period.
2   The various sessions should be taken by members of the management team assisted as necessary by external specialists.

Index

ABSENTEEISM, REGULATION OF 142
Activity sampling 36–7
    drawbacks 36
Added value 39, 82–3, 92–5, 109–10
    calculation 109
    choice of ratio and use as index
        112–14
    effectiveness of index 93–5
    establishment 109–10
    variables affecting ratio 92–3
Alcan Industries Ltd, reduction of
    numbers on shift work 136
Amalgamated Engineering Union, and
    full-time officials 188–9
Annual improvement factor 110,
    114
Appeals system 7, 155, 160–2
    recommended procedure 237–9
Area of investigation 23–5
Associated Industrial Consultants Ltd
    80, 204, 212
Attendance standards, definition of
    142
Attitude surveys 51–8, 164–6, 169
    analysis of results 53–7
    examples 52–8, 204–9
    questionnaires 51–3
    random surveys 51
    shop stewards and 51, 165–6
    willingness to participate 56, 58
Avon Rubber Company Ltd and
    theory *Y* 10

BALL, PROFESSOR R J 39
Barnes, M 138
Barnes, Ralph M 36

Behavioural scientists 11
Benign environment
    school 9
Bonuses 91
    curves 125–7
Boundary disputes 157
Break-even charts 41–5
Britain on Borrowed Time (Jones and
    Barnes) 138
British Industry Week 142
British Oxygen Company Ltd 1
Business Ratios (*Ball*) 39

CANNON, LES 183
Carrington agreement 165
Classical productivity agreements
    1–2
    beneficial results 2
    limitations 2
    special features 2
Command system 7, 154, 156–7
    chain of command 156
    meetings 156
Communications 151–62
    and problem-solving 152
    appeals system 7, 155, 160–2
    as basis of good management 152
    characteristics of system 152
    command system 7, 154, 156–7
    consultation system 7, 155–6,
        158–9
    design of system 154–62
    face-to-face contact 152
    information about agreements
        168–71
    interlinking between groups 152

255

Communications *continued*
  negotiation system 7, 154–8
  principles 151–4
  requirements of system 153–4
  structure 7
  suggestion schemes 159–60
Comprehensive agreement, contents of
    6–8
  communications structure 7
  fringe benefits 7
  rational wages system 6–7
  role specification and measurement
    6
  rules and procedures 7
  security of employment 6
Computers 65, 100, 102–4
Consultation system 7, 155–6,
    158–9
  departmental productivity panels
    159
Contracts of Employment Act 1963
    145, 147, 216, 220, 228
Controlled day-work, *see* Measured
    and controlled day-work
Coryton agreement 132–3, 136
Costs and costing 46–9
  effect of incentive payments 124–7
  labour costs 46–8
  of labour turnover 59–60
  of overtime 133–4
  of rationalising wage structure
    119–24
  reduction of overall costs 48–9
Coventry mutuality systems 75–7
Current wage systems 73–85
  graded hourly rates 80–1
  measured and controlled day-work
    77–80
  payment-by-results 73–7
  plant-wide incentive schemes 81–5

DAY-WORK, MEASURED AND CONTROL-
    LED 77–80
Decentralised structures 25–6
Design of components of scheme
    96–114
  job evaluation 96–104
  share-of-prosperity element 109–14
  variable element 104–9
Devising productivity agreements
    131–43
  labour flexibility 138–40

reactions to work study 140–2
reduction of overtime 132–6
regulation of lateness and
    absenteeism 142
revision of working hours 135–8
staff status and fringe benefits
    142–3
Differentials 90, 96, 116
  importance of 87–8
  in existing wage structures 66–8
Direct consensus method of job
    evaluation 100–4, 164
  analysis of results 102–4
  assessment procedure 102
  comparison forms 101
  effectiveness 104
  job descriptions 101
  judges 101–2
  paired comparisons 100–1, 104
  ranking forms 102
  representative sample 101
  use of computers 100, 102–4
Dispute procedures 240–1
Docks, restriction practices in 138
Donovan report 24, 153–4, 188
  see also Royal Commission on Trade
    Unions and Employers' Associ-
    ations

ECONOMIC ANALYSIS AND COSTING
    41–9
  break-even charts 41–5
  sales and market trends 45–6
Electrical Trades Union 183
Employee motivation and industrial
    relations 9–18
  basic assumption and concepts
    10–11, 16–17
  "benign environment" school 9
  changing views 9–11
  hierarchy of needs 11–13
  motivation–hygiene theory 13–15
  positive policy 176–7
  restructuring 17–18
  supportive relationships 15–16
  theory X 10
  theory Y 10, 16, 17
  traditional concepts 9–10
Equitable Payment (Jaques) 87
Esso Petroleum Company Ltd 1
  Fawley agreements 9, 132, 138,
    165

FACTOR PLAN METHOD OF JOB EVALUATION 97–8
Fairfield experiment 139
Fawley agreements 9, 138, 165
  and reduction of overtime 132
Feasibility study 21–49, 166, 169–70, 178–9
  area of investigation 23–5
  economic analysis and costing 41–9
  creation of industrial relations policy 26–8
  large company problems 25–6
  production analysis 29–40
  schematic representation 22–3
  scope and organisational implications 21–8
Financial ratios 39–40
  added value 39
Firestone Tyre and Rubber Company, joint disciplinary committee 142
Foremen:
  role of 176, 180–1
  training 181, 252–4
(Samuel) Fox and Company, consultation and negotiation systems 156
Fringe benefits 7
  and staff status 142–3
Full-time trade union officials 183, 188–90

GRADED HOURLY RATES 80–1
  appeals committees 81
  assessment form 212–15
  responsibility of foreman 80–1
  subjectivity of assessment 81
Graded payment structures 96–7
Grade structures 110–19
  basis of new proposals 118–19
  career progression 116
  cost 119–24
  defined 116–18
  numbers of grades 117
  rank order of jobs 99, 118
  simplicity 117
Gunter, R J 136

HAWTHORNE EXPERIMENTS 50
Heiland, R 36

Herzberg, Frederick 11
  and motivation–hygiene theory 13, 163, 176
Hierarchy of needs 11–13
  basic needs 11
  egotistic needs 11–12
  safety needs 11
  social needs 11
Hinderances 29, 197–9
  see also Restriction practices
Hourly rates, graded 80–1
House journals 153
Human Side of Enterprise, The (MacGregor) 10

ILFORD LTD, AND PROBLEM SOLVING 3
Imperial Chemical Industries Ltd, and motivational theories 13
Implementation of productivity agreements 166–71
  communication of information about agreement 168–71
  in departments and sections 171
  meetings with shop stewards 167, 170
  programme 166–8
Implications for management 175–82
  foreman's role 176, 180–1
  managerial initiative and industrial relations policy 177–9
  new management style 179–80
  positive motivational policy 176–7
Implications for trade unions 183–90
  impact on natural agreements 183–4
  role of shop stewards 183–8
  role of union officials 183, 188–90
Incentive schemes 68–9, 116, 166
  effectiveness of current schemes 68–9
  incentive payments and costs 124–7
  plant-wide schemes 81–5
Information about agreements 168–71
  and meetings with shop stewards 170
  at feasibility study stage 169–70
  booklet for employees 170
  implementation in departments and sections 171
  written communications 170

Institute of Personnel Management 145
Introduction to Shift Working (Ministry of Labour booklet) 136

JAQUES, DR ELLIOTT; AND TIME-SPAN OF DISCRETION 99
on differentials 87–8
Job enlargement programmes 139–40
Job enrichment 13
Job evaluation 96–104, 110, 164, 169
  direct consensus method 100–4, 164
  employees' involvement 99–100, 104
  factor plan method 97–8
  graded payment structures 96–7
  need for acceptability 99
  new approach 99–100
  rank order of jobs 99, 118
Joint consultation 158–9
  committees 2–3
  machinery 58–9
Joint disciplinary committees 142
Jones, Aubrey 74
Jones, G 138

LABOUR COSTS 46–8
  increases 47–8
  ratio to sales or added value 82–3, 92–5
  reduction 46, 48
  restructuring of system 47
  semi-variable nature 82–3
Labour flexibility 138–40
  job enlargement programme 139–40
  restriction practices 138–9
Labour turnover:
  analysis of incidence and pattern 59–60
  costs 59–60
Large company problems 25–6
Lateness, regulation of 142
Learning curve effect 77
Likert, Rensis 11
  and supportive relationships 15–16
Line management 179
  and personnel departments 178–9

Line system 154
  see also Command system
Lupton, Professor Tom 77–8

MACGREGOR, DOUGLAS 10–12
  theory X and theory Y 10, 16
Machine speeds and productivity 37–8
Managerial initiative and industrial relations policy 177–9
  personnel departments 178–9
Managers and Shop Stewards (Marsh) 175–6
Manpower planning:
  and security of employment 144–50
  definition of 145
  economic necessity for 145
  redundancy 144–5, 147–8
Market trends 45–6
Marsh, Arthur 175–6
Maslow 11–13
Measured and controlled day-work 77–80
  and control information 78, 80
  difference between measured and controlled 77
  Philips premium payment plan 78–80
  preparation for use 78
Measurement of Responsibility (Jaques) 87
Merit payment 80–1
Michigan University, Institute for Social Research 11
Ministry of Labour Survey of shift work 136–7
Mobil Oil Company Ltd, Coryton refinery agreement 132–3, 136
Model remuneration principles 86–95
  added value component 92–5
  common expectations 86–7
  importance of differentials 87–8
  jobs or roles 86–7
  share-of-prosperity element 90–2
  variable element schemes 88–90
Motivation, *see* Employee motivation
Motivation–hygiene theory 13–15, 163, 176
  job enrichment 13
  satisfiers and dissatisfiers 13–14
  work simplification 15

MTM   36, 78, 142
Multiple regression analysis   38–9, 83, 200–3
  areas of application   203
  calculation   203
  number and type of variables 202–3
  procedure   201–2
  sources of data   202
  theory   200–1
  validity   203
Mutuality systems   75–7
Myers, E Scott   13

NATIONAL AGREEMENTS   183–4
  Handbook   240
National Board for Prices and Incomes, *see* Prices and Incomes Board
National Coal Board, and absenteeism 142
National Economic Development Office, estimate of costs of labour turnover   60
National Union of General and Municipal Workers   185
Negotiation of productivity agreements   163–8
  attitude surveys   164–6
  different approaches   165
  job evaluation   164
  meetings with shop stewards   167
  objectives   168
  programme   166–8
  share-of-prosperity element   164–5
Negotiation system of communications 7, 154–8
  and boundary disputes   157
  joint committees   157–8

OVERTIME   167
  and productivity levels   134–5
  cost of   133–4
  employees' attitudes to   134
  overtime bans   134
  reduction   132–6

PARKINSON COWAN APPLIANCES LTD 109
Pay bands and performance   108–9

Payment-by-results systems   24, 73–7
  Coventry "mutuality"   75–7
  criticisms   74, 76
  effectiveness   73–5
  learning curve effect   77
  need to analyse current systems 74–5
  problems   76–7
Payment-by-results Systems (Price and Incomes Board Report)   74, 210–11
Personal assessment schemes   90
Personnel departments   178–9
Philips Electrical group, premium payment plan   75–80
Plant-wide incentive schemes   81–5
  advantages   85
  criticisms   84
  implications   84–5
  motivating factors   85
  multiple regression analysis   83
  physical output measures   83
  profit sharing schemes   82
  ratio of labour costs to added values 82–3, 92–5
  Rucker plan   81–2
  Scanlon plan   81–2
  statistical techniques   83
PMTS (predetermined motion–time systems)   34, 36, 79, 142
Premium payment plan (Philips Electrica lgroup)   78–80
  contracted performance   79–80
Prices and Incomes Act   177, 192
Prices and Incomes Board   2, 5, 75, 112, 192
  and work study   30, 34
  report on job evaluation   97, 99
  report on payment-by-result systems 74, 76–7, 210–11
Printing industry and restriction practices   138
Problem-solving committees   3
Production analysis   29-40
  activity sampling   36–7
  financial ratios   39–40
  hindrances   29
  machine speeds   37–8
  measurement requirements   29–33
  measurement techniques and methods   30, 32–6
  multiple regression analysis   38–9
  work content   30–2

Production analysis *continued*
  work study 31, 34
Productivity agreements 131–71
  and new system of wage payment
    244–51
  checklist for proposals 242–3
  communications 151–62
  devising the agreement 131–43
  manpower planning and security of
    employment 144–50
  negotiation and implementation
    163–71
Productivity bargaining in depth 1–8
  "classical" bargains 1–2
  contents of comprehensive
    agreement 6–8
  definition of productivity bargaining
    1–2
  joint consultative committees 2–3
  need for comprehensive approach
    2–6
  problem-solving committees 3
  rationalisation of wages 3
  understanding of motivation 5
  wage bargaining 1
  wage–work bargaining 1–2
Profit sharing schemes 82, 91
Protective practices, *see* Restrictive
  practices

RADICE, GILES 185
Rank order of job 99, 118
Rationalisation of wage structures 3,
  6–7, 115–27, 167
  basis of new grade structures
    118–19
  cost 119–24
  defined grade structure 116–18
  incentive payments and costs
    124–7
Redundancy 141, 144–5, 147–9,
  216–23
  voluntary procedures 148–9
Redundancy Payments Act 1965 145,
  147, 149, 216, 218, 220
Remuneration principles, model
  86–95
Restrictive practices 29, 138–9
  in docks 138
  in printing industry 138
  in shipbuilding industry 139
Richardson, W J 36

Role specification and measurement 6
Rootes Group Ltd 76
Rota systems, revision of 135–6
Royal Commission on Trade Unions
  and Employers' Associations 24,
  192–3
  on communications systems 153–4
  on role of shop stewards 183,
    185–6
  on role of union officials 183,
    188–9
  on wage bargaining and wage–work
    bargaining 1
Rucker plan 81–2
  ratio of labour costs to added value
    82

SAFETY NEEDS 11
Sales trends 45–6
Satisfiers and dissatisfiers 13–14
Scanlon plan 81–2, 92–3
Security of employment 6, 167
  and manpower planning 144–50
  development of plan 146–50
  importance to employees 144
  model plan 216–23
Share-of-prosperity element 90–2,
  116, 164–5
  annual improvement factor 110,
    114
  choice of ratio and use as index
    112–14
  design 109–14
  economic argument 91–2
  establishment of added value
    109–10
  models 110–12
  sociological argument 91
Shell Company, Corrington works
  agreement 165
Shift work 135–8
  attraction of labour 136–7
  changes in systems 135–6
  consultations with employees
    137–8
  greater use of plant and machinery
    136
  reasons for introduction 135–7
  reduction in overtime 136
  sociological implications 137
Shipbuilding industry and restrictive
  practices 139

Shop stewards   21, 23–4, 51, 61, 165–7, 170, 179
  and attitude surveys   51, 165–6
  and grade structures   118
  opportunities for talking to members   187
  regularisation of position   186
  relationship with managers   185–7
  role   183–8
  training   187–8
Single or multi-plant agreements   24–5
Sociological analysis   50–61, 204
  attitude surveys   51–8
  joint consultative machinery   58–9
  labour turnover   59–60
  recourse to established grievance procedure   60
  types of dispute   60
Staff status and fringe benefits   142–3
Steel Company of Wales   1
Steele, P M   36
Suggestion schemes   159–60
  recommended constitution   233–6
Supervisors, *see* Foremen
Supportive relationships   15–16

Teabreaks   2
Teach Yourself MTM   2
  (Steele)   36
Texas Instruments, and motivational theories   13–15
Theory X 10, 16, 17
Theory Y 10, 16
Time-span of Discretion   99
Trade unions and implications of productivity agreements   183–90
Trades Union Congress   188
Training:
  of shop stewards   187–8
  of supervisors   181, 252–4
Tube Investments Ltd:
  Tubes Ltd productivity agreement   136

United States:
  behavioural scientists   11
  plant-wide incentive schemes   81
United Steel Companies   156

Variable element system   88–90, 167
  accuracy of measurement   106–7
  and differentials   90
  design   104–9
  measured and non-measured systems   90
  pay bands and perforemance   108–9
  personal assessment schemes   90
  predictability of earnings   89–90
  proportionate payments   107
  relation to job holder's contribution   89
  reward for achievement   89
  stabilisation   107–9
  yield index   105–6

Wage analysis   62–9
  aspects to be covered   62
  differentials in existing structure   66–8
  effectiveness of existing incentive schemes   68–9
  major components of gross earnings   64–5
  most suitable reference period   63–4, 116
  need for detailed analysis   62–3
  technique   63–5
Wage bargaining   1
Wage rationalisation   3, 6–7, 115–27
Wage–work bargaining   1–2
  categories   1
Whitley Committee   151
Wilde, Oscar, quoted   48
Wilson, Harold   138
Women employees and shift work   136–7
Work content   30–2
  BS 3138 scale   32
Work measurement techniques   30, 32–6, 140–2
  diagram   35
  employee and union suspicion   140–1
  MTM   36, 78, 142
  PMTS   34, 36, 79, 142
  work study   34, 140–2
Work Sampling (Barnes)   36
Work Sampling (Richardson and Heiland)   36
Work simplification   15

Work study   1, 31, 34
  employee and union reactions
    140–2
  fears of redundancy   141
Workers' Educational Association
  187
Working hours, revision of   135–8

Works productivity council:
  notes for chairmen, representatives
    and electors   230–2
  recommended constitution   224–9

YIELD INDEX   105–6